Own Your Life Again!

The Five-Step Method

For Controlling

Depression, Anxiety and More!

Judie C. McMath, MS, BHRS

DEDICATION

To all those for whom happiness has been elusive.

CONTENTS

ACKNOWLEDGMENTS

I would like to thank Dr. Joseph Mercola and his website because that is where I learned about energy medicine in the first place. Thanks also goes to Sonia Galindo for the beautiful cover photo. Most importantly, I would like to thank my husband for encouraging me to reach for the stars.

CHAPTER ONE

SEVEN-YEAR DEPRESSION SUFFERER
GETS RELIEF IN 10 MINUTES!

At a recent party I attended I met a woman we'll call Margaret, a friend of the hostess who had been suffering from severe long-term depression for over seven years. In an attempt to help Margaret stop focusing on her depression, the hostess had persuaded her to come to this party, but she was obviously sad, preoccupied and very ill at ease. After talking with Margaret for a while, I learned that she had been to therapy and taken antidepressant medication, but was not able to get significant relief. She had spent so much time in therapy that she was aware of her emotional issues, but was unable to believe that any treatment would help her since nothing she had tried so far had been effective.

I pulled out a folded up copy of a handout that I use in my classes which just happened to still be in my purse from the last class I had taught. I outlined the Five-Step Process, briefly explained it to her, and asked her if she would be willing to try it when she got home that night. She agreed, but added that she didn't have much hope that it would help. I asked her if I could call her the next day to see how she did. I also gave her my phone number in case she needed my help while she was going through the process.

First thing the next morning she called me before I could call her. She was exuberant! I could hear the excitement in her voice.

"It's gone" she shouted into the phone. I can't believe it. It's gone!"

Margaret recounted enthusiastically how she had gone through the process once and had felt significant improvement the first time. She went through it several more times until suddenly, as she described it, "It was like the sun came out." Suddenly she knew she was getting better. What seven years of therapy had not been able to accomplish, Margaret did on her own in less than 10 minutes.

Does this surprise you?

The "traditional" treatments for depression and anxiety are weeks or years of counseling or "talk therapy" and/or medication. These treatments often fail because they don't address the <u>root cause</u> of the illness. "One of the most challenging problems in depression research and clinical practice is refractory -- hard to treat -- depression. While approximately 80 percent of people with depression respond very positively to treatment, a significant number of individuals remain treatment refractory. Even among treatment responders, many do not have complete or lasting improvement, and adverse side effects are common. Thus, an important goal of NIMH research is to advance the development of more effective treatments for depression -- especially treatment-refractory depression -- that also have fewer side effects than currently available treatments" (1).

Most treatment programs hem and haw and say that the cause **may be** a chemical imbalance in the brain, genetic factors, or traumatic experiences in your past. These are not the causes, although they may be contributing factors.

Consider this:

If it was a chemical imbalance, the medication would make it go away.

If it was genetic, you wouldn't be able to do anything about it.

If it was caused by trauma, well, we've all experienced trauma of some kind in our lives. So why don't we all have depression and anxiety?

Let's say that two people get into a swimming pool together. Neither of them have ever had any traumatic experiences with water. One of them gets pushed under by a friend and comes up laughing. The other gets pushed under and when he come sup he suddenly has a fear of water that makes him avoid swimming pools for the rest of his life.

What is the difference between these two people?

A simple illustration. In your home, you probably have a breaker box with fuses. When you get too much stress on one electrical line, the breaker trips and the electricity goes off. Nothing on that line will work until you unplug some things from the line and flip the breaker back on. Then your electricity flows again and your television, blender and computer will work again.

The same thing happens with your body. Something happens to make you experience a loss of control in your life. This puts stress on your body's electrical system. If its more stress than you can handle, you experience a short-circuit in your energy system. Things stop working right in your body and mind. You begin to feel depressed or anxious, and it begins to affect your life in a negative way. Half of all depressed people have high levels of cortisol, the stress hormone secreted by the adrenal glands. Depression and anxiety are often linked reactions to stress or trauma (2). Loss of control is one of the biggest stressors.

Now all you have to do is reset your body's breaker switch and make sure your body's electrical system isn't overloaded in the future!

Sound Easy Enough?

I have created a **Five-Step Process** that will take you through what you need to do to accomplish this. Each step is explained simply and is easy to understand. The process is a concrete tool to reduce or eliminate depression, anxiety and much more. In fact, the Veteran's Administration is currently in year two of a five year study on the effectiveness of using a form of this method for treating Veterans. The preliminary findings have been that 89% of those using the technique experience significant relief from their symptoms. In May 2012 the American Psychological Association endorsed a form of this technique as an "evidence-based" treatment modality, which means studies show it to be safe and effective. It won't take you weeks or years of therapy to see some results, and it can be done at your own pace in the privacy of your own home.

Can I do counseling too?

Of course, you are always free to use these techniques in combination with anything you are already doing. Many people find that they get significant relief using the technique on their own without any help from anybody else. Even though I trained to be a counselor, I found this technique to be much more helpful than traditional counseling, so it's not surprising then that when I experienced depression for myself, I looked for a way to help myself rather than seek out a therapist.

How I Overcame My Own Depression and Anxiety

I grew up in a broken home. My mother and father divorced when I was a very young child. I have only three memories of ever seeing my father, and I had no brothers or sisters. All my life we lived with my grandparents. We never had a home of our own, and the only way I knew what a "normal" family looked like was from watching television. I'd watch television shows like "The Waltons" or "Eight is Enough" and I'd see a mother, father and lots of brothers and sisters. I realized I was missing something. I didn't let it bother me on the surface, but deep down inside there was a longing there.

After I graduated from high school, I went on to college because all my friends were. But I really did not want a career. I wanted one thing: to get married and have babies. I wanted to re-create the family I missed out on. I started out with a major in computers, but my heart wasn't in computers. I was also in the choir and found that through music, in some indirect way, I was able to express the feelings that were in my heart that no one was interested in hearing about in my real life. The joys I felt, the sorrows I lived with, the deep longings in my heart. Even though the words to the songs I sang weren't speaking to these particular things, the emotions in the songs poured out of me. I switched my major to music.

My voice teacher was a wonderful man. When I was in his studio fro my vocal lessons, he recognized something in me. He encouraged me, told me how smart I was, and helped me to realize things about myself that nobody else had ever seen in me or expressed to me. Very soon we became close and he became like a father to me. For the first time I knew what it was like to be nurtured by a parent, and I was even more saddened by what I had missed out on by not having a father. For two years, I depended on him to feed me emotionally and help me catch up on all those years of feeling alone. Due to the traumas in her life, my mother was also very emotionally distant, and for the first time I knew what I had been deprived of.

Just as I was starting to feel alive and whole again, my new father figure was forced to move to another city because of his work. I was devastated when he left, feeling empty and alone again. After three years of music education, and four years of college total, I changed my major to English. I began writing words where there once was music. I had things inside me that needed to be said, but nobody was listening.

I'd spent four years in college without finishing a degree, and although the nurturing I'd received had partially assuaged the loneliness I felt, it wasn't enough. I longed for a relationship that would fill me up, emotionally and spiritually. I had gone to church almost all my life, and had a close relationship with God, but this did not fill me like I thought it should. My relationship with God was unsatisfying. At the time I did not realize it, but many other people experience this dissatisfaction with their relationship with God. Unfortunately, they are often shamed into not admitting it, or the church makes them feel like there is something wrong with them because there certainly couldn't be anything wrong with God. How wrong they are.

I met a man at my church. We were both lonely and looking for companionship, and we turned to each other in a time of need. He said he was looking for someone to share his life with, and he wanted that person to be me. I was so thrilled that someone wanted me that I threw myself headlong into the relationship. I finally had someone to spend my time with, someone who said they WANTED to be with me. I wasn't really attracted to him, but I WAS attracted to the fact that someone wanted me. I was being offered a relationship and I wasn't going to turn it down. We were married before the end of the year, and one year later I gave birth to our first child. Finally, I had the life of my dreams, or so I thought.

I was deeply in love with my baby, but not my husband. Still, I loved nurturing my child, keeping house, and welcomed any loving actions from my husband. I tried to be a good wife. I performed all the obligations of a dutiful wife. I expected in return all the obligations of a dutiful husband that the church had taught me to expect. I had been taught, "You take care of the children and everything inside the home and your husband will bring home a paycheck and take care of everything outside the home like the cars, the lawn, etc. You take care of him and he will take care of you."

The only problem was, my husband hadn't the foggiest idea how to take care of me. Oh, he did bring home a paycheck, but that was it. He didn't have any idea how to nurture me emotionally, and three months after we were married, the engine of my car almost blew up because he never checked the fluids or the oil levels, and my radiator was dry. He couldn't fix anything around the house, and he had a terrible temper. So I learned to take care of myself, physically and emotionally. I had to. I stopped expecting him to take care of my needs, and if anything needed fixing, it just had to wait until I could pay someone to come and repair it. I never shared bad news with him if I could avoid it because I didn't want to be subjected to his angry outbursts. As the years went by, I depended upon him less and less, both physically and emotionally. I basically only depended on him for my physical survival. He brought in a paycheck and took care of our survival needs, but that was all. I continued to try and be a dutiful wife as much as possible, but inside I began to resent the fact that I didn't receive the relationship the church promised me, and even though he wasn't meeting any of my personal or emotional needs, I was still supposed to submit to him because he was the "head of the house."

Then he lost his job. He was out of work for eleven months before he found another one. By that time, our two children were 11 and 16, and we had started homeschooling. When we first married, I had told him up front that I wanted to be a stay-at-home mom because I believed it was important that my children have me there when they were growing up. I told him I wanted to cook and clean and teach our children and make a home. He knew this from the beginning. But at some point, he began to resent the fact that I didn't bring in any income. When he lost his job, I was forced to seek employment because our family could not survive without it, but it didn't feel good inside because I was no longer fulfilling the calling that I felt. He finally found another job making more money than we'd ever had. I finally felt it was safe to quit my job and go back to nurturing our home, which I did. I also started my own business which I did from our home in my spare time. It felt good to be able to supplement our income while still staying true to my calling of being a stay-at-home mom. But it was not to last. After working at his new job for two years, my husband lost his job again because the place he worked was closing. His employer helped everyone who worked there find jobs. He only kept that job two weeks and then quit. The next job he only kept for three days. Then he was out of work for three months, and after finally finding another job, quit it after only three months. This pattern was becoming of concern to me.

During the last three months that my husband was out of work, we sold almost everything we owned to keep food on the table. My husband saw our possessions disappearing one by one, and he knew why. Finally we had no furniture in our living room, and our only possessions were our computers, clothing, beds and dishes. I had to have my computer to run my business, so I couldn't sell it. Our house became empty inside, and so did I. I couldn't understand why he kept quitting these jobs. I talked with him about our financial situation one day because he complained about how we never had any money. I showed him on paper how we didn't have enough money coming in to pay for all our bills as well as his hobbies. I told him that I was writing a book and was pretty sure I would be able to sell it. I asked him to give me a little more time to get some more money coming in, and then he could quit his job. I told him I understood what it was like to work at something you didn't enjoy, and I would support him in finding something else, but asked him to please not quit his job until he'd already found another position somewhere. I thought he understood and agreed to this, but the next day after we had this conversation, he came in and said he'd put in his two week notice at his job.

I was stunned. He knew we were in a precarious financial situation, and I'd specifically asked him not to quit his job until he had another one lined up, but he paid no heed to what I'd said. When he said he was quitting, something inside me snapped. I told him I just couldn't talk about this now, and left the house immediately. I was not receiving any emotional support from him in my life, and now I was receiving no financial support either. I had no belongings left to sell. What did he expect us to do?

I decided that I needed to do something to let him know how serious I felt the situation was. By this time the kids were 17 and 22 years old. I explained the situation to them, and they agreed we should move out. We packed our things and moved in with a relative. I had always been the one to do the budget and pay the bills, and I decided that he needed to know first hand how hard it was to struggle to make ends meet, so he should have to live in the house and grapple with these bills alone.

At first, he agreed to find another job, live in the house and work on paying the bills. By this time, I had dreams of becoming successful with my books and moving to Colorado and buying a house there. I wanted to live somewhere beautiful and spend my life doing something I enjoyed and felt called to do. He said he didn't want to do that, and he decided to move back to his home state and live near his mother, brothers and sisters. He said he wasn't interested in following me to fulfill my dreams, even though I had followed him everywhere the Army had moved us for years. I thought that was very unfair, especially since he didn't currently have a job and since I had followed him through our whole marriage wherever he needed to go. He said he didn't want to work on any of his "issues" so he left. That meant I had to move back into our house and find a job quickly so I could make the house payment. I found a job and within two weeks was bringing in a full time income. But it still wasn't enough to pay all the bills, so both my kids had to get part-time jobs to help pay the bills.

Now you are probably wondering why I had to tell this big, long story - it's so you can understand how the depression developed and why. I now have compassion for people with depression, and for people who commit suicide or just run off, desert their families and are never seen again. It's because they have no hope.

Every day, I got up and went to a job that paid the bills but was meaningless. I cried when I had to go to work every day because I saw no purpose to my job other than just to make a paycheck. I am a person who feels it's important that someone fulfill their calling, and I've always been a nurturer, but every day I was forced to do work where I felt all I was doing was running on a treadmill, like a rat in a cage. I learned first-hand about what the term "rat race" means. I thought to myself, now I know why people go out and get drunk on the weekends, because they are so miserable during the week. I know why people get depressed - they feel they have no control over their situation, and they have no hope that things are going to change in the future. It took all my strength to stay out of the doldrums, but sometimes I wasn't strong enough. Sometimes depression would just hover over me, like a predator waiting to strike.

I walked around like a zombie, feeling like there was always a dark cloud over my head. The rug had been pulled out from under me, and I was falling, and trying to grab onto anything that would stop the fall, but there was nothing to grab onto. No matter what I did, nothing helped. I felt so lost and helpless. I don't know how I functioned during that time. I went to work, acted normal, but inside I was dying. I couldn't enjoy my friends or anything I used to like doing. I developed depression because I perceived that I was not able to control my life. Everything seemed out of control. Most emotional problems and mental illnesses develop as survival mechanisms when people experience a loss of control in their lives. I don't know where I found the strength, but finally, I made a decision: I chose not to feel that way anymore. I had to find something to help myself.

Now, I didn't feel better overnight, but when I made the decision to take **100% responsibility for the way I was feeling,** it was the turning point. I chose not to blame my husband for leaving and for not knowing how to meet my needs. I chose not to mourn about the life I didn't have. I and only I made the choices which defined my life. No one else could define me. **I could change the definitions**.

As we all know, it's easy to make a change in your beliefs intellectually, but depression and anxiety are two of those stubborn things that just don't immediately go away because you change your thoughts. People wouldn't spend years in therapy and still be unable to get relief from their symptoms if that was the case. However, most people don't know about this simple technique which most therapists are not trained in, which can quickly cause a shift in your feelings and make getting rid of your depression seem like a possibility rather than a distant dream.

After several recurring bouts of depression, I learned about an innovative new method for bringing balance back into my life. It works both by changing brain chemistry, balancing electrical pathways, and helping the individual to reprogram themselves with healthy ideas and feelings. I learned that by using this technique, I could change some of my feelings immediately, right then and there, and others I could change over a period of a few hours or days. Now I had a tool that would radically change my feelings and I was the one in control of it. **Now, I was the one with the power!**

So I had made the choice to change my life, and I had found a tool to help me change it. My depression happened because I felt I was not in control of my life, and had no hope that I could change things. Now I needed to take action to make sure this loss of control didn't happen again.

From my depression and anxiety, I learned that I needed to take action in order to start feeling better. I needed to begin to restore my feeling of control over my life by discovering **concrete ways** of changing my feelings and my responses to stressful situations. My loss of control happened because I was depending upon someone other than myself to make me happy. It also happened because I was depending upon someone else to provide for my financial needs, and I had not developed my talents so that they could support me. I had a vision of what I wanted for my future, but I didn't see any way to get it. I worked all day and when I came home, I was too tired to enjoy my children or my life outside work, but yet there was still work to do at home that had to be done. I thought to myself, how do people do this, work at a 40-hour-per-week job without going crazy? You are constantly moving from one thing to the next, and you have to keep moving or you won't get through it. I didn't want to continue this kind of life. So I decided to make the things I really enjoy doing into a career.

I developed a website, wrote these books, started selling them in eBook form, then as paper books, and then I started doing personal coaching and teaching the techniques that had helped me take my life back. I knew that other people who had similar problems would be interested in how I was able to get rid of my depression and finally control my life again. I could control my schedule so I only worked when I wanted to, and when you develop a system where you do your work once and get paid for it over and over again, this frees you from having to run on that treadmill anymore. I could finally see how I could someday have the life I wanted. I had hope again.

But unless I had first used the **Five-Step Process** I would not have even been able to believe that hope was possible. When you are depressed, sometimes you can't believe that anything will help you, and you don't have the energy to try. This process helped me to see clearly that there was hope, and it controlled my negative emotions so I could experience some joy in my life again. Once I experienced joy again, I had the energy to go on.

Actually, our **Five-Step Process** will work even if you don't believe you have a problem, don't believe it will help you, or don't understand the core issues of the problem, which is different from traditional counseling, in which they try to get you to see the connections between your present circumstances and your past experiences. It's helpful to see this causal link, but **not always necessary in order to fix the short circuit in your body and change your negative emotions.**

So what did I do again to restore control of my life, get my hope back, and begin to change my depression?

First, I took responsibility for my life. Only I could change it. I couldn't depend on others to do it for me (I also could not depend on God to do it for me – see Appendix).

Second, I used **The Five-Step Process** to correct the disruption in my body's energy system which was causing the depression to persist, despite my best efforts to change it.

Third, I made changes to my life that helped prevent me from experiencing further loss of control, and thereby helped prevent the situations from recurring which had caused the extra stress on my energy system.

When I used **The Five-Step Process**, some of my feelings changed almost immediately. This gave me reason to believe that other more persistent feelings could be changed eventually if I just worked on them. I know it may seem hard to believe, but you REALLY can get a significant change in your feelings the FIRST day you use this process. I am living proof, as well as the thousands of others who have received hope and help from this process.

References:

1. http://psychcentral.com/disorders/depressionresearch.htm
2. Epperson, C. N. et al. 1999. Gonadal steroids in the treatment of mood disorders. Psychosomatic Medicine 61:676-689.
3. http://imagineyousuccessful.com/2012/05/15/break-out-the-champagne-eft-apa-validatede/

CHAPTER TWO

DON'T BELIEVE IT WILL WORK?

I don't blame you for being skeptical. If you've already tried all the traditional treatments and they didn't work, you probably don't believe there is anything that can help you. You can receive hope that it can help you by listening to the following stories from those who have changed their lives using this process.

Cindy: "I come from a family in which my mother was very critical and did not ever show physical affection or touching. I was always made to feel like I was not good enough. Then I married my husband, and thought things would be better. At one point, he stopped working and the responsibility for providing for our family fell totally on me. We had two children, and I had to work, care for the children and the home, everything. He did not help at all. He was also verbally and physically abusive. He would yell at our children, and throw things. The children were showing signs of being traumatized by this as well. He would demand I give him money so he could go out and do the things he wanted, but he never contributed to bringing in any money. I am an artist and was trying to develop my art into a career, but had to stop to take a menial job making minimum wage so I could put food on the table. My self-esteem was pretty low. I sank into a depression because I just couldn't see how my situation would ever change. I felt pretty hopeless, and the only thing that kept me from suicide was the thought of leaving my two children alone with him. After using The Five-Step Process, my depression began to lift. My feelings of powerlessness stopped, and I quit feeling afraid to try and step out on my own. I can't describe it, but after just two rounds of using the process, I felt this electricity go right through me, and my fear turned to anger and then to resolve. I wasn't going to let him do this to me! One reason my self-esteem was so low was because I hated myself for being depressed, anxious and not capable of standing up for myself. The Five-Step Process helped me change that opinion of myself, so I felt strong enough to do whatever it took to get back on track. I do it all day long, every time something negative comes into my head, I don't let it stay there. Using the process put me back in control of my life. It's simple, only takes a minute or two, and you can do it anywhere, anytime. I don't know where I'd be without it."

Note: Filling out the worksheets, which is the preliminary work, may take a few extra minutes to do in the beginning. However, the process itself, after learned, can be done very quickly. You carry it with you wherever you go as a tool for life.

Karen: "I have been depressed from the time I was 10 or 11 years old. When I was young, my father shared with me that when I was born, he really wanted a boy. I always tried to please him but never felt good enough. Even though I am a professional and do well at my job, I never felt successful. I have gotten into a lot of trouble, getting into relationships with men because I just crave male attention. My father pretty much ignored me in my childhood, and even though my superiors at work give me praise and have confidence in my abilities, I often felt like a failure. I had many unrealistic expectations of myself, and when I didn't think I was fulfilling them, I'd become sad and depressed. It made it hard to function in my job, I didn't want to get out of bed in the morning to go to work. When I started working with the Five-Step Process, within minutes I began to see that I really was successful. It's like a light bulb turned on suddenly for me. I laughed out loud, because I couldn't believe I had actually accepted this negative picture of myself when the evidence was so obviously to the contrary. There's something about depression, it makes it impossible to accept or even in some cases, to see the truth about yourself and your situation. Using the Process brought almost instant improvement. I still had some issues to work through, but now I could see clearly what to do and didn't feel immobilized by my depression."

Doug: "I was depressed for many years. It was hard for me to admit I was depressed, because it seemed like a women's thing. You know, more women have depression than men, and plus we are supposed to be strong and macho and not let stuff like this affect us. I was having relationship problems and my job was in danger, and I began to feel sad and then pretty much without emotion all the time. I thought the problems with my relationship and job were the core issue, so I started addressing these with The Five-Step Process, but quickly found that there were other, deeper issues from my childhood. My mom left us and I always blamed myself for her leaving, thinking it might have been my fault. I always felt my family didn't love me because they blamed me for my mother leaving, although this was not the case. As soon as I started working with the Process, it's like the clouds suddenly lifted. I could suddenly see that it wasn't my fault. I had been too young, and the things that happened weren't my responsibility. Funny how I couldn't see those things before. I felt so much better immediately, I only had to use the Process again briefly a couple of times, and my depression has not returned."

Sandy: "I started using the Five-Step Process for my postpartum depression. During the birth process, a lot of things happened that made me frustrated and angry. I felt fine while I was standing or walking around, but when I would sit or lie down, I had extreme pain and felt that things just weren't right. However, when I got to the hospital they insisted I lie in bed with a fetal monitor on. I tried to tell them that I couldn't do this because it was too painful, but they said it was hospital policy and I had to. Like a good little girl, I did as I was told. The pain was so bad, I had to have an epidural which I didn't want. I had wanted to have totally natural childbirth, as I believe that the drugs given during labor and delivery are not good for the baby. So right away, I felt bad about myself because I allowed myself to be given this drug. As a result of the numbing effects of the epidural, I could not push my baby out and ended up with a c-section. They decided to do one because my baby's heart rate was dropping during contractions, and they feared the cord was being pinched or was around the baby's neck. When the baby came out, the cord was not around the neck, and after some research, I concluded that when I sat or laid down, that pinched the cord and was causing not only my pain but deprived my baby of oxygen. I hated myself for giving in to the doctors and nurses who made me feel like I could not refuse the procedures they were forcing me into. I wanted to be in control of what was being done to me, but felt powerless to make anyone listen. After I went home from the hospital, I had a hard time taking care of my baby. I was sad and depressed most of the time. It took everything I had to make myself get up and take care of her when she cried. I didn't shower, didn't eat right, could barely function to get dinner on the table or the dishes washed. I was generally a wreck. I knew what happened wasn't my baby's fault, but I felt so guilty when I was around her. It just reminded me what a bad mother I was, and how I should have stood up to those doctors and nurses. After using the Five-Step Process the first time, I felt better, but I still needed to use it every day to deal with my guilt. When I used it, I was able to more effectively care for my daughter, as well as my own bodily needs. It helped my immediate symptoms to get better, but I had to use it consistently every day for about two weeks before I really feel like the depression completely started to lift. My hormones could have had something to do with it as well. Even though it took about two weeks for my depression to improve, I am so thankful for the Five-Step

Process and the techniques I have learned to help myself. They wanted to give me antidepressants but I was breastfeeding and didn't want the baby to get those drugs in my milk, so this was the perfect alternative for me."

Jessica: I am a very creative person. I am an author, write music, and am successful business wise. I recently decided to branch out and use my talents in some new ways, but found many obstacles to doing this, which made me frustrated and even question the usefulness of my talents. I became depressed, physically ill, and pretty much useless. I belong to a large church which has some very impressive technologies to help people with self-improvement, and I spent thousands of dollars working on these processes (which right there should have told me something, a church that charges you money to receive help?). I improved in many areas, but the depression remained a problem. I didn't want to take drugs, so was looking for some other way. A friend of mine who had used the Process recommended it to me, and I have to say, I probably wouldn't have tried it at all if she hadn't given it such a high recommendation. It IS very hard to believe that something so simple can help you. It's like someone giving you a spoon and telling you that in five minutes you can empty the ocean, one spoon at a time. It just doesn't make sense, but I can tell you from personal experience, it works. After just the first use of the Process, I saw significant improvement. I had enough improvement that I could start using my creative gifts again. I use the Process every day to balance any negative experiences, thoughts or feelings that I have. Most days I have no problem at all. A couple of times the depression seemed to come back, but I was able to dispel it quickly and easily, and I am now confident that I will always be depression-free. I now know which things in my life are likely to cause such a relapse, and I deal with those events before they are able to cause a problem. I realize, it's not the things that happen to me, it's how I react to them, it's whether or not I take control of the situation or let the situation control me. With this simple Five-Step Process, I am in control."

Tammy: Last year I helped to organize a fund raiser for a charity I am involved in. I really believe in the work this charity does here in my local community, and they are well known here for their work. But no matter what I tried to do, I couldn't seem to get a good response from the community. The people I asked to speak cancelled, people who had promised to donate time, products or services simply decided they couldn't do it after all, and I wasn't getting the response I wanted from those I had invited. It looked like the whole thing was going to fall apart. I started to get depressed about the whole thing, and pretty much began to doubt my own abilities, which is unusual for me, I am usually very confident. I came home one night, upset and disgruntled, and got into a fight with my partner. No matter what she did that evening, I kept getting upset about it, picking a fight. I finally left the house and just drove around for a while, ending up out at the lake. I parked my car and got out. I walked out into the lake, and it kept getting deeper and deeper. Pretty soon it was over my head, and I was treading water. I remember thinking, all I have to do is just stop treading water and it will be over. I can't believe I had these thoughts, I've never been prone to being so negative about myself, and I've never had thoughts of suicide before. It was like I just couldn't see anything good about myself, the negativity just overpowered my sense of logic. I felt like I was under a black cloud emotionally. As I had that thought that all I had to do was just stop treading water, I really became alarmed by that thought. One part of me was really miserable, and the other part of me was standing to the side, saying "What are you doing? You don't want to kill yourself!" But the negative part seemed stronger, pulling at me. Then I remembered, I had been at a friend's house one night with a terrific headache, and she had taught me this technique that she uses to get rid of pain and emotional issues. I used the technique for only one minute, and my headache left and never returned. In a desperate moment, I decided, right there in the water, to try the technique again. I wasn't sure if I even remembered it correctly, but I started doing what I remembered. I went through the technique once, and all of a sudden it just dawned on me how ludicrous this whole situation was. What was I doing out there in the water? I swam back to shore, got out of the water, and sat on the hood of my car to dry off. While I was sitting there, I did the technique several more times. Each time, things became clearer and clearer. I saw that I had made some incorrect assumptions which led me to take some actions which were negatively affecting the fund raiser. I saw very clearly what I needed to do to correct these problems. I also saw that I had been wrong in how I had treated my partner, that I had been picking fights and she was not at fault. I went back home, apologized to my partner, and the next day I started to work on the problems with the fund raiser. To make a long story short, it was a huge success, even more than I could possibly have imagined it could be. I went back to my friend who had briefly shared the Process with me, and had her teach it to me more fully, and this time I paid close attention. Not only did the Process get rid of my depression and suicidal thoughts, it helped me to see key areas in my life where there were problems, and gave me insight and solutions as to how to fix those things. I am so grateful I had a friend who shared this with me. What's more, I now teach the Process to everyone who has any kind of problem that I think it could help with, which is pretty much any problem. Try it yourself, you'll see."

Shawn: I have been depressed for years, with anxiety and some phobias. I've worked on it with traditional therapy and had become aware of some of my issues, but it wasn't really helping get rid of the depression. I was afraid to touch anything with fur, whether it be an actual live animal, a fur coat, or even fake fur. It just gave me chills, I'd start to sweat and feel dizzy. I had tried to work on this for so long, and I was very depressed because I didn't know where this fear had come from, or how I'd ever get rid of it. Sometimes if I saw someone across the room wearing fur, or sometimes even a picture of an animal or something in a movie, I'd just start to panic. I was never able to go out and do anything because I never knew when I'd see something that would trigger it, so I stayed home most of the time. I sank into a deep depression, and even antidepressants didn't help. I was surfing the internet, trying to find some help, and came across this process. I actually just was so sad and hopeless, I wanted something to help me feel not so depressed because that was almost as bad as the actual phobia. But every time I tried to think about anything happy, these sad, hopeless thoughts would come back. I tried using the process on my depression, but for some strange reason, as soon as I started trying to do that, some thoughts started flashing through my mind. I started remembering things that happened many years ago that I guess I had blocked out of my mind. I remembered an incident of being sexually abused by a relative, and it happened on a bear skin rug. I suddenly felt absolutely wild with panic, like it was happening all over again. I started to use the Process just to calm myself down emotionally. Suddenly, as I went through the process, right in the midst of feeling this panic, I could suddenly see clearly that there WAS a possibility that I could heal from this. The depression had a cause, and now I knew what it was. I suddenly felt so full of hope and light, even there in the midst of the horrible realization of what happened to me. I can't describe it, how even though I was crying and shaking and was incredibly upset, another part of me was rejoicing. I knew from that moment on I would get rid of the depression. In fact, after I calmed down and stopped crying and shaking, I felt incredibly at peace and no longer depressed. Now, I still had to deal with the sexual abuse issues, but no more phobias, and no more depression."

Chris: "When I was pregnant with my first child, I gained a lot of weight, which did not come back off after the birth of the child. I became very depressed because I was unhappy about my appearance, and I couldn't seem to lose the weight. I started to feel very resentful toward my child because of it. I knew this was not logical, but just couldn't help it. I started smoking cigarettes too, partly to deal with the stress of feeling so down on myself, and partly because I had heard it might help me lose weight, but it didn't. I just kept eating more and more, because I figured, since I can't lose this weight, I might as well eat what I want. So I had two addictions. I got more and more depressed, and it was affecting my job and relationships. I used the 5-Step Process to deal with my depression, and found that one of the issues causing the depression was not just the weight, but the fact that the man that got me pregnant deserted me and I never saw him again. I thought the depression was about the weight, but it was about the desertion. When I started to feel less depressed about that, the weight just started to fall off. I also was able to get rid of my craving for cigarettes with just one session using the Process. So it works not only for depression, but addictions as well."

Candace: I had been a Christian for many years. I was completely devoted to my religion, my spiritual practice, my faith and my God. But it seemed like God repeatedly let me down. The Bible said that God would not give you anything you could not handle, but I repeatedly felt overwhelmed, prayed for help, and never received any. I was desperate to hear something from God that would give me guidance, supernatural intervention, or just plain give me some clue as to what I could do to help myself. No help came. I looked in every direction. I was repeatedly told just to "pray and have faith" but that did not seem to be working. Why wouldn't God give me the answer? If he knew my heart, he must have known just how much I wanted help and how much I wanted to preserve my relationship with him. Then I heard about the Five-Step Process. People said it was "of the devil" because I could use it to "heal myself." And we're not supposed to depend on ourselves, but God. Well, I didn't care. I needed help and nobody was offering me anything else. All the laying on of hands and praying was not helping. I felt depressed, alone, and disillusioned. I tried the Five-Step Process and after using it just a couple of times, I felt better. This was absolutely phenomenal! There was something that could help me. I learned that all the answers I need are inside me, and nowhere else. Not only did the Process help me heal myself, but if I ever needed the answer to a question, the Process provided a way for me to find the answer. I finally came into my power and experienced the sweetest, purest love imaginable – without a god, real or imagined.

Want to try it for yourself now?

You could be Depression-Free in the next 30 Minutes.

CHAPTER THREE

THE FIVE-STEP PROCESS
WHICH CAN CHANGE YOUR LIFE FOR GOOD

IDENTIFY THE PROBLEM

LOSS OF CONTROL ACTION SHEET

EMOTIONAL IDENTIFICATION ACTION SHEET

APPLY ACCU-BALANCING TECHNIQUE

TAKE ACTION TO PREVENT FUTURE LOSS OF CONTROL

Just a few ground rules for using this method

Set aside an afternoon to do this. It may only take a few minutes, or you may find after you get into it that you want more time to think about it.

This experience will be different than anything you may have done in counseling to try and alleviate your depression or anxiety. Don't try and judge how well you are doing by how long it takes you to complete the process. Some people may take ten minutes to get relief, some may take an hour, a day, or a week. Most experience a significant amount of relief at first, and then more and more as the days and weeks go by. Some people actually eliminate their problem altogether in the very beginning of the process. Whatever happens is right for you, and you can't say that because one person felt better after ten minutes, that if it takes you two hours, there must be something wrong. The stress that is on your electrical system is different than anybody else's, so try not to judge or criticize yourself.

This process works whether you believe it will or not. It's also **not** about trying to figure out what you did wrong, if anything. It's simply about identifying the emotions you are currently having which you find negative or unpleasant, and thinking about those emotions while you go through the physical process of correcting the electrical imbalance.

This is a process which, once you have learned it, you can use it daily to keep your energy system balanced and in great working order.

Typically, a person experiences a loss of control as a result of a particular experience in their life. For example, say a person learns they have a serious illness. They are taking medical treatments, but don't seem to be getting any better. They may feel they have no control over the situation they are in. Depression is very common in situations where there is hopelessness because a person does not feel they can do anything about their circumstances.

As an example, my friend Gina's father passed away. There were quite a few issues to be dealt with surrounding his estate and decisions that needed to be made regarding money and property. Every time Gina tried to think constructively about what to do, she felt sad, overwhelmed, and would get a migraine headache. After showing her how to do the process, her headache pain completely disappeared. She also realized that the sadness and feeling of being overwhelmed were gone, and she could think about her father's affairs without experiencing these negative emotions. She was able to make the appropriate decisions without feeling hopeless and overwhelmed, and she was able to experience missing her father without it triggering any depression or anxiety.

One of the biggest predictors of learned helplessness and depression is blame. The list of symptoms of depression includes feelings of worthlessness or guilt, but the blame we put on ourselves that causes us to feel guilty or worthless is actually a huge factor in our development of depression. You will see that in one of the steps in the Accu-Balancing Technique, you are required to construct a sentence that affirms that you love, accept and forgive yourself. That gets rid of the blame and guilt, and it triggers your electrical system to correct any energy imbalances which are causing negative feelings as a result of that blame and guilt. You will learn a technique to help your body repair these electrical pathways and restore your sense of well being.

The next five chapters will take you through each of the five steps, one at a time. You will be amazed at how simple the process is! It has been proven successful in thousands of clinical cases, yet it requires no formal training to learn to do it, and works with just about any emotional, performance or health issue. In fact, this process usually **works where nothing else will**.

First you will **identify the problem** (depression, anxiety, or some other emotional issue). Then you will complete the **Loss of Control Action Sheet**, and the **Emotional Identification Action Sheet**. You will then have the information you need to actually **apply the ABT technique**. After applying the technique, you should see some noticeable change in the way you feel. If you feel the situation is resolved, you are done, except for **taking action** to change the circumstances of your life so you don't experience another loss of control.

If your feelings have not changed as much as you'd like, you go back to your Emotional Identification Worksheet and apply the technique to each emotion listed there. If that doesn't give you the results you want, you then go to the Loss of Control Worksheet, and apply the technique to each situation listed there. Normally this process will at least touch on all the emotional issues which could possibly be interfering with your life, unless you have left something out of your worksheets when you filled them out.

Most people are able to complete this process themselves. If you feel you need support while going through this process, please call our office support number to talk with a practitioner, or make an appointment for a telephone session in which we will go through the process with you, or help give you some insights into other ways to apply the process to your particular situation. Our phone number and email address are listed in the Appendix of this book.

Now Let's Get Started!

CHAPTER FOUR

IDENTIFY THE PROBLEM
THAT IS CONTROLLING YOU

Step One of the Five-Step Process

Some of you will already have been to a physician, psychiatrist or counselor, and will already have been given a diagnosis of depression or anxiety. If that is the case, then you have probably already completed **Step One** of the **Five-Step Process.** Many of you, however, have chosen not to go to a "professional" because, for one reason or another, you do not want to expose your problems to scrutiny by others. For some people, this represents another "loss of control" issue.

How can seeking help from a professional represent a loss of control, especially when the individual involved made the choice of their own free will to go seek assistance? Many people do not like getting involved with the mental health system. They have had past experiences where they have not been treated with respect and dignity. They have been given inappropriate medications or inappropriate amounts of medications. They have been treated by burned out mental health workers who aren't able to have the compassion or empathy that they should have, who don't really understand people with emotional issues, and don't really want to take the time to learn. When people seek help and then feel that their trust has been violated because the people taking care of them do things that are unpleasant or inappropriate, this creates another loss of control issue which can intensify the original problem they sought help for. Also, some people feel that, once in the mental health system, a record of their problems follows them and they lose control of who knows about their situation.

For those people who aren't sure whether they have a problem or not, and don't want to go to a professional in person, you can visit this website link:

http://www.diagnose-me.com/

The Diagnose-Me website uses a sophisticated computer program called the Analyst, which has the combined knowledge of many doctors and researchers. It looks at your health from many perspectives, and shows the full reasoning behind its findings. Many doctors actually use the website to help them make diagnoses because it's impossible for one doctor to keep up with all the research and treatments available. After answering the questions about your physical and emotional symptoms, the results can be sent to an anonymous email address. Nobody ever need know that you filled out the questionnaire. You can give a false name if that makes you feel safer. A preliminary, free summary is sent to your email address. There are also three paid reports which you can order.

Computer Only Analysis - $25.00 - A highly detailed analysis, NOT reviewed by a doctor.

Standard Report - $47.00 - A highly detailed analysis, reviewed by a named, licensed doctor, before being sent to you.

Full Report - $77.00 - A named, licensed, doctor will review and summarize your report, as well as providing his or her own insights, and you will be able to contact them to ask questions at no additional charge.

These were the prices at the time of the printing of this book. These prices are subject to change without notice and we are not responsible for the prices.

When you are sent your free questionnaire, it states that they are not allowed to discussed prescription drug treatments in the free report (because this requires a doctor's recommendation), so the report discusses other options such as diet and lifestyle changes. If you purchase a report which is reviewed by a doctor, at that time you can get information about prescription drug options, if that is what you desire. As always, the choice and control is yours. I bring this website to your attention because it is another way that you can deal with your problems in the privacy of your own home, where you retain the control, if that is what you desire. If it's important for you to know that you have a clinical diagnosis, this is a good option. If you already know you have depression or anxiety, or some other emotional issue, you can continue on to **Step Two** of the **Five-Step Process**.

Let's take a minute to review the most common symptoms of depression and anxiety.

Common Symptoms of Depression

- feeling miserable and sad
- exhausted, feel like sleeping a lot of the time, hard to get out of bed
- feelings of anxiety, or emptiness
- feelings of hopelessness, pessimism
- the smallest tasks seem extraordinarily difficult
- you find it difficult to think clearly
- feelings of guilt, helplessness, worthlessness
- more irritable or angry than usual
- changes in appetite, such as not eating/losing weight, or overeating/gaining
- loss of interest in activities that used to be pleasurable
- you feel that life is unfair
- early morning waking, insomnia, disturbing dreams
- you sometimes feel anxious
- constantly worried about what may or may not happen
- difficulty making decisions
- physical problems such as headaches, back pain, digestive disorders
- thoughts of suicide

Do you have at least at least five of these symptoms that have lasted for more than two weeks continuously? Or at least three that have persisted mildly for at least two years? Then you could have some level of clinical depression.

Common Symptoms of Postpartum Depression

Up to 80% of postpartum women and some fathers suffer from postpartum depression. A mild form includes symptoms that typically last from a few hours to several days, and include tearfulness, irritability, hypochondriasis, sleeplessness, impairment of concentration, isolation and headache. This mild form is NOT considered clinical depression, and usually disappears in a few days or weeks. Even though this is not considered a clinical disorder, the 5-Step Process will also help alleviate the discomforts of this mild form. More severe clinical postpartum depression can include the symptoms of major depression, can last longer and be more severe.

Risk factors for Postpartum Depression

* Prenatal depression, i.e., during pregnancy
* Low self esteem

* Childcare stress
* Prenatal anxiety
* Life stress
* Low social support
* Poor marital relationship
* History of previous depression
* Infant temperament problems/colic
* Maternity blues
* Single parent
* Low socioeconomic status
* Unplanned/unwanted pregnancy
* history of genetic mental illnesses
* substance abuse
* former childbirth issues

Other than a previous history of depression, in my opinion, the most prevalent cause of postpartum depression is former childbirth issues. Hospital birth is very disempowering, and women often experience loss of control issues as a result of being forced to accept routine hospital procedures or having to endure humiliating treatment. I have often found Post Traumatic Stress Disorder to develop as a result of these loss of control issues.

Common Symptoms of Anxiety Disorders

- excessive worry and tension
- recurrent nightmares or flashbacks to traumatic events
- restlessness or a feeling of being on edge
- muscle tension, headaches, sweating, nausea
- tiredness
- trouble falling or staying asleep
- trembling, being easily startled
- difficulty concentrated
- need to go to the bathroom frequently
- irritability
- feeling of electrical current or energy rush going through body
- ice cold sensation or feeling of ants crawling over the body
- feeling detached from the body or as if things are not real
- breathing difficulties, choking sensation
- low back pain, aching jaw, sciatica
- racing, pounding heart

Do you have the majority of these symptoms, more days than not, for the past 6 months or more? You may have some form of Anxiety Disorder. The service provided by the Diagnose-Me site is no substitute for a visit with a qualified, licensed health care professional. Follow your gut instinct. If you feel you need to see a qualified health provider, please do so.

Whether your depression and anxiety meet the criteria for a clinical diagnosis or not, you can still use The Five-Step Process to alleviate your symptoms.

As you are going through the **Five-Step Process**, keep a notebook handy and jot down any questions that you think of. Call our office at **580-483-4767** or email us at: unhinderedliving@gmail.com

YOU are close to success now. Even though you may not understand yet how it is going to happen, it is looming on the horizon. You are about to touch it.

Congratulate yourself on having that courage!

CHAPTER FIVE

BE YOUR OWN EXPERT THERAPIST

THE LOSS OF CONTROL ACTION SHEET
STEP TWO OF THE FIVE-STEP PROCESS

Please list painful memories. Here are some of my examples:

Memory	How old?
Disappointment with husband because he didn't meet my needs or take care of me.	Age 23
Husband blows up, yelling and cursing at me and the kids in the car, had to go inside a friend's home and pretend everything was all right.	Age 31
Husband keeps losing or quitting jobs. Bills past due, collection agencies calling.	Age 40-46
Physical exhaustion and emotional hopelessness from working 40-hour-per-week job.	Age 46
Despair from feeling I would never be able to make any of my dreams come true.	Age 46

Now It's Your Turn

Loss of Control Action Sheet

Memory	How Old?
_____	_____
_____	_____
_____	_____
_____	_____
_____	_____
_____	_____
_____	_____
_____	_____
_____	_____
_____	_____
_____	_____
_____	_____
_____	_____
_____	_____
_____	_____

Continue on another piece of paper if needed. Think of as many as you can. Now, what did you lose control over?

Think about each of these memories. We don't have negative emotions unless we have experienced a loss of control. What loss of control does each of these memories represent? In the examples I gave:

I was not able to control whether or not I received the love and nurturing I needed.

I was not able to control my loneliness by having a relationship with someone who met my needs.

I lost my feeling of safety and self-respect from husband's outbursts of anger and yelling.

I lost a feeling of security when husband quit jobs.

I lost hope for the future because of I couldn't see how I'd ever get able to pay my bills and be able to stop working at a tiring, dead-end job.

List Your Loss of Control Issues Here

_____

_____

_____

_____

_____

_____

_____

_____

CHAPTER SIX

TIME TO PLAY THE NAME GAME

THE EMOTIONAL IDENTIFICATION ACTION SHEET
STEP THREE OF THE FIVE-STEP PROCESS

Now that you have identified the situations in your past which you perceive as causing you a loss of control, please try to give a name to the emotions you experienced during those situations, as well as the emotions you experience now when you think about them.

Please use two different colored pens. For emotions you experienced in the **past**, use a blue pen. For emotions you are experiencing in the **present**, either now or on a regular basis, use a red pen.

After circling the emotions that are troubling you, place a small number 1 by the one that is troubling you the most, then 2 by the next most troublesome one, and so on until all the circled emotions have a number by them. Knowing which emotions you are feeling, and which ones you want to change, will be important information in **Step Four - Applying ABT.**

Emotional Identification Action Sheet

Acceptance, Agitation, Alarm, Amusement, Anger, Angst, Annoyance,
Anticipation, Apprehension, Apathy, Awe
Bitterness, Boredom
Calmness, Comfort, Contentment, Confidence, Courage
Disgust, Disappointment, Discontentment, Desire, Delight
Elation or Euphoria, Embarrassment, Envy, Ecstasy
Fear, Friendship, Frustration
Glee, Gladness, Gratitude, Grief, Guilt
Hate, Happiness, Homesickness, Honor, Hope, Horror, Humility,
Impatience, Inadequacy, Irritability
Joy, Jealousy, Kindness
Loneliness, Love, Lust
Melancholy, Modesty
Nervousness, Negativity, Nostalgia
Pain, Patience, Peace, Phobia, Pity, Pride
Rage, Regret, Remorse, Resentment
Sadness, Self-pity, Shame, Shyness, Sorrow, Shock, Suffering, Surprise,
Suspense
Terror
Unhappiness
Vulnerability
Worry
Yearning
Zest

CHAPTER SEVEN

CHANGE YOUR LIFE
NOT NEXT WEEK, NOT NEXT MONTH, NOW!

STEP FOUR - APPLY ABT (ACCU-BALANCING TECHNIQUE)

The Accu-BalancingTechnique is a unique, easy-to-use method for bringing immediate change to your depressed or anxious feelings. It is a clinically-proven procedure with a higher rate of success than traditional talk therapy or medication.

ABT balances the body's electrical system. It utilizes the same energy points as acupuncture - but WITHOUT using needles. Instead, we just use two fingers of one hand to gently but firmly TAP on the appropriate energy points. In fact, we get better results with just tapping than the acupuncturist does with his needles.

While going through the tapping procedure, at some point you will notice a distinct energy shift within your body. Those who have used the method report an almost immediate change in their feelings. **Whereas things might have felt hopeless before, now they feel more hopeful. Now, you are able to believe that success is in sight.**

Is there any basis for the idea that stimulating the body's electrical system can elevate your mood?

In 1988, the FDA approved Vagus Nerve Stimulation as a treatment for epilepsy. In this treatment, a pacemaker-like device is implanted in the chest and sends intermittent electrical stimulation to the vagus nerve, which stimulates certain areas of the brain. Patients who took this treatment for epilepsy also reported a significant elevation in mood, prompting research as to whether or not Vagus Nerve Stimulation could be used as a treatment for depression. At this time it is considered an effective treatment for depression that has resisted other forms of treatment.

By doing the Accu-Balancing Technique tapping procedure, you are safely and effectively stimulating your body's electrical system so that you can remove or lessen negative emotions, elevate your mood, and increase positive emotions and general well-being. A major advantage of ABT over Vagus Nerve Stimulation is that no surgery is required to implant anything. ABT is a totally non-invasive process. An additional feature of ABT which Vagus Nerve Stimulation does not have is that with ABT you are able to pinpoint which emotions you want to change and target particular past events or situations which have caused a problem for you. You will actually be able to measure a change in your feelings immediately after using the technique.

In order to measure this change in feelings, before doing the procedure we ask you to rate your starting intensity. On a scale of 0 to 10, how intense is your feeling of _____ ? Perhaps you have chosen to work on your feeling of hopelessness. Please use the rating scale of 0 to 10 with 1 being barely noticeable, 5 being moderately annoying, and 10 being unbearable. You may, of course, use all the numbers in between 0 and 10. You will choose which emotion to work on based upon the answers you circled on the **Emotional Identification Action Sheet.**

Before starting the tapping procedure, you must decide which emotion to start working on first. Look at the **Emotional Identification Action Sheet** and see which circled emotion has a red number 1 next to it, meaning that this emotion is the most troubling to you. You will start with this emotion.

You must construct a **start-up phrase** using this emotion. Examples:

"Even though I am feeling this hopelessness, I thoroughly and completely love, accept and forgive myself."

"Even though I can't believe I'll ever be able to get rid of this hopelessness, I thoroughly and completely love, accept and and forgive myself."

"Even though I don't know how to get rid of this hopelessness, I thoroughly and completely love, accept and forgive myself."

ABT Tapping Points

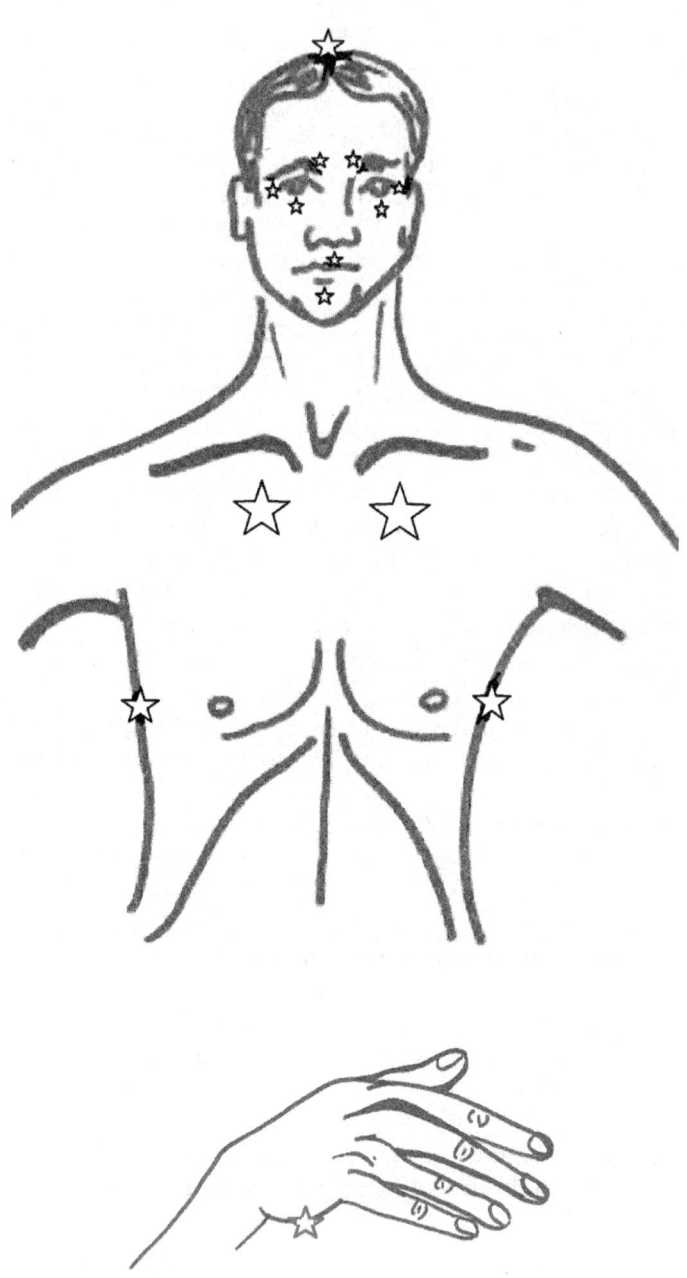

Or in another form:

"Even though I feel hopeless, I choose to believe there is hope."

"My hopelessness is now changing to optimism."

"I choose to believe that my hopelessness is gone."

The purpose of constructing these phrases is to help you tune in to the problem so that the tapping procedure will help your body to correct the energy imbalance associated with that particular emotion or event.

Once you have chosen the appropriate phrase, look at the tapping points chart. You have a choice of two different points to tap on using the start-up phrase. You can choose the karate chop point on the side of the hand, which is the midpoint between the wrist and the bottom of the pinkie, or you can choose the tender spot on either side of the chest, underneath the collarbone. Choose which one you are going to use, and begin tapping on that point with the first two fingers of your hand (either right or left) and while you are repeatedly tapping, say the startup phrase three times. By doing this, you are giving your body heads up about what electrical pathway you want to repair.

So, do it now. On the lines below, write the start-up phrase you have chosen.

_____

_____

Now, tap on the karate chop point or tender spot, saying it three times.

You are now done with the start-up. For the rest of the procedure, you don't have to say the whole sentence; you will shorten it to one or two words so it's just a prompting phrase. For example, if your start-up phrase was "I choose to believe my hopelessness is gone" then your prompting word would be "hopelessness." For the rest of the procedure, you simply say "hopelessness" when you tap on each point, and think about what that hopelessness feels like. Really tune into it.

Now, start tapping using the index and middle finger of either hand. It's good to use your dominant hand (the hand your write with) if you can, but you don't have to. Tap firmly but not hard enough to hurt yourself. Tap approximately 5-7 times per spot, but you don't have to concentrate too much on how many times you've done it, just tap several times. The important thing is to tune in to how you are feeling while tapping by saying the prompting word or phrase. For this example, it's the word "hopelessness." Here is the order of the tapping points. Do them in this order, from the top of the head down, and ending back at the top of the head again. As you tap on each point, you will say the word "hopelessness" or whatever your particular prompting phrase is. Each of these points occurs on both sides of the body. You don't have to tap on both sides. Pick a side, or switch back and forth. It really doesn't matter, as long as you hit each point. You can use one hand on one side of the body, or both hands and tap on both sides at once. It's your choice. Tap firmly, but not hard enough to hurt or injure yourself.

Order of Tapping Points

Top of Head
Eyebrow
Side of Eye
Under Eye
Under Nose
Chin
Collarbone
Under Arm
Back to Top of Head

OK, that's one round. Take a deep breath, and let it out. Now, rate your intensity again. How intense is your feeling of _____? Remember what your number was before? Is it the same or lower now? Many people find that the intensity of the hopelessness, or whatever emotion they were feeling, has dropped significantly by just doing this one round of tapping.

If you did **not** drop to zero intensity yet, do another round of tapping. Change the start-up phrase to indicate that, although some of the emotion has left, there is still some remaining. For example: "Even though I still have some of that hopelessness left, I thoroughly and completely love and accept myself." Then, your prompting phrase will be "remaining hopelessness." Now do your second round of tapping using that phrase. Do it now.

Now rate the intensity of your emotion again. Has it dropped some more? If it has dropped to zero, it's gone! **Congratulate yourself!** If it's not all gone yet, try one more round. Change the prompting phrase. Try "It's all gone!" Tap on each point and when you say it, raise your voice a little and do it with **gusto!**

Now rate the intensity again. If it's all gone, you are ready to go on to another emotion or issue. If it's down to a 2 or 1 and you can't get it to drop anymore, still **Congratulate yourself** on reducing it significantly and giving yourself relief, and hope!

Now, when an issue drops to 2 or 1 and stays there, that is often a sign that there is some other underlying issue that this emotion is associated with that must be dealt with. So, think about that emotion, and look back at the **Loss of Control Action Sheet.** Look at those events which caused you a loss of control, and determine which of them is associated with this hopelessness you are trying to get rid of. When you think of a particular incident in your life, does it trigger these feelings of hopelessness, or whatever emotion you are working on? Once you have identified which event to work on, construct your start-up phrase like this: "Even though I'm so sad about my sister dying and I can't seem to focus on anything in my life, and everything seems hopeless, I thoroughly and completely love and accept myself." Since the event that triggered this hopelessness appears to be the death of the sister, make that your prompting phrase: "sister dying," or whatever your issue is.

Write the issue here

_____

Say that every time you tap on the tapping points from the top of head down. First, rate the intensity of how you feel about your **issue,** whatever the issue is. **Then start tapping.** You can do up to three rounds on this issue, changing the phrasing slightly each time. Do it now. Now rate your intensity again. Is it 0? 1 or 2?

If you still aren't at 0, you can change the issue again. Go back to the **Loss of Control Action Sheet** and pick the next event which caused you to experience this emotional issue. If it's not on the sheet, think back in your mind until you find an issue that seems to bring out this emotion in you. You can keep trying this, tapping on each issue and changing the prompting phrase, until you are at zero.

What if I don't get to zero, even after changing the focus of my tapping several times?

If you've tried different emotions and issues, changed your start-up phrases and prompting phrases, and still can't get it, there are some other things we can try. One technique is called the **Floor to Ceiling Eye Roll**. Sit in your chair with your back straight, looking straight ahead. Now, without moving your head, lower your eyes so you are looking at the floor. Now, to the count of six, raise your eyes slowly so that you are sweeping them upward from the floor all the way to the ceiling. Count to six as you do this, so when you say the word "six" you are looking up at the ceiling. Remember not to move your head, only your eyes. While you are doing this, you should be thinking about the emotion, event or issue that you haven't been able to eliminate. Try it now.

Now rate your intensity again. Is it 0? If you are still not able to say that you have eliminated your emotion or issue, it may be because a part of you does not feel it is **safe to change** this now. Take both hands and, if you have long enough hair, push the hair back behind your ears. When you did that, you probably used an up, over and behind motion, sweeping the hand up, over and behind the ear in a circular pattern. Over the top of and down behind the ears are some tapping points, so I want you to tap on an imaginary line which contains these points, up over and down behind the ears. While you do this, think about the issue you have been unable to eliminate, and say out loud, over and over, "It is now safe to get over this problem." Do this over-the-ear tapping procedure at least five times, or more if you want. You are now eliminating your body's fight-or-flight response as it has been associated with this memory.

Before you can lay the foundation for building good, positive thoughts, beliefs and emotions, it's important to **Forgive Yourself**. Place your hand over your heart, rotate the hand in clockwise motion, and repeat, "I forgive myself. I have done the best I know how with........" As an example,

"I forgive my sister for dying (or whatever your issue is)."

"I forgive other people (name them specifically) because they......"

"I forgive myself for not changing this pattern sooner."

Now, to re-program your body so that it feels safe to get over this problem, take both hands and go to the top of your forehead. At the top right and top left of the forehead, there are two energy centers. Begin to massage these energy centers with a circular motion, and while you are doing this, say out loud things like:

"Even though I miss my sister, I am feeling better about her being gone.
"The feeling of sadness is passing."
"I am feeling hopeful again."
"I am able to accept her passing."
"I am feeling peaceful again."
"My feelings for my sister will not interfere with my life anymore."

Make up as many sentences as you can that express positive change. These are the feelings or perspectives that you **want to develop**. As you repeat these sayings and massage the forehead energy points, your body will tune in to your needs and desires, and will begin to wipe out the old feelings and program in the new ones.

Now, take a deep breath. Let it out. Rate your intensity level once more. Some people who have tried this procedure and have not been successful in reducing or eliminating their emotion or issue, find that having a session or two with a trained **ABT Practitioner** can make them feel safe enough to let go of the problem. We do these sessions in person or over the phone. If you feel you would benefit from such a session, please contact us at

The Center for Unhindered Living
unhinderedliving@gmail.com
580-483-4767

Energy Toxins

Occasionally, if a person is unable to get their intensity level down to zero, they might be affected by an energy toxin. This is a substance which is interfering with your body's electrical system. By eliminating these energy toxins, you may be able to eliminate the blockage you are experiencing. Some of the more common energy toxins are:

caffeine
sugar
wheat
corn
eggs
soy
chicken
calcium
milk
synthetic Vitamin C
synthetic B-Complex Vitamins
peanuts
titanium
artificial sweeteners
minerals
heavy metals
petrochemicals
pesticides
vaccines

There can also be energy toxins in your cleaning products, perfumes, personal care products and or anything that contains a lot of chemicals. Cigarette smoke can have them, as pretty much all addictive substances have them. Sometimes pesticides on foods are the culprit. Do you have dark circles under your eyes, an unexplained rash on your face or ears? These are often signs of the presence of energy toxins in the body that are not being eliminated. Even if you don't have these symptoms, there can be an energy toxin interfering with your electrical system. The experience of many ABT practitioners has been that people with depression or anxiety often have an energy toxin in the detergent they use to wash their clothing. Ecover and Seventh Generation are good non-toxic cleaning products, or you can make your own. See our website page "House Beautiful or House Deadly" at

http://unhinderedliving.blogspot.com/2014/09/house-beautifulor-house-deadly.html

Start by eliminating one of these items at a time and then see if the tapping is more successful for you (or eliminate them all at once and then add them back into your diet one at a time). After you have discovered which toxin is the culprit, totally eliminate it from your diet or stop using the product that contains these chemicals. Some people can be extremely sensitive to certain chemicals and not even know it. Just eliminating something from your diet or surroundings is often enough to make your tapping sessions successful. Occasionally, you will need to use ABT to clear the energy toxin so that you won't be susceptible to it again. This can be done by doing the tapping using a start-up phrase like, "Even though my body reacts badly to wheat, I choose for my body to clear any wheat sensitivity" or "I choose for my body to stop reacting negatively to wheat" or however you want to phrase it. Then, after eliminating your energy toxin, try tapping on the original issues you were working on to see if you can clear them now. If you are not sure if a particular substance is an energy toxin, it won't hurt to go ahead and tap on that substance anyway, just in case.

Now, how successful have you been?

Issue Clearing Record   Date _____

Emotions currently troubling me   **Events currently troubling me**
that I have cleared   **that I have cleared**

_____   _____
_____   _____
_____   _____
_____   _____
_____   _____
_____   _____
_____   _____
_____   _____
_____   _____
_____   _____

Emotions troubling me from   **Events troubling me from the**
past that I have cleared   **past that I have cleared**

_____   _____
_____   _____
_____   _____
_____   _____
_____   _____
_____   _____
_____   _____
_____   _____
_____   _____
_____   _____

Make a copy of the three worksheets, three hole punch them, and put them in a notebook. Keep track of the issues you have cleared. You can often look back at these records and see a pattern of emotions and issues which you can work on further at a later time.

CHAPTER EIGHT

TAKE ACTION TO PREVENT FURTHER
LOSS OF CONTROL – STEP FIVE

In my own situation, I felt that I had to remove myself from my relationship with my husband in order to restore control of my financial situation and my self-respect. Later on, I felt I needed to remove myself from the 9-to-5 rat race in order to prevent my depression from being triggered again.

How do we know that feelings of loss of control can lead to depression? Think about it. Things are happening to you that you can't control. You have tried every solution and nothing seems to work. You see no evidence that your situation will ever improve. You basically give up any hope that things will change. This is called Learned Helplessness. In a study by Mark D. Pagel, et al., researchers studied spouses who were caring for a husband or wife with Alzheimer's disease. The study showed that feelings of loss of control were consistently related to depression (1). In Martin Seligman's model of learned helplessness, depression is triggered when three criteria are met:

- the individual is aware of uncontrollable factors in their environment
- the individual views the situation as unchangeable
- they blame themselves for their helplessness – internal attribution (2).

If you completed the **Loss of Control Action Sheet**, you will have identified issues in your life which make you experience a loss of control. When you experience a loss of control, it makes you feel like you cannot do anything to change your circumstances. Using ABT can help you feel differently about that, so that you can feel empowered to take action.

What Kind of Action Should I Take?

Most often, this involves removing yourself from situations and relationships which are making you feel stressed, uncomfortable, or placing obstacles in the way of your peace and happiness. In most cases you don't have to end the relationship, just set some boundaries for yourself, and don't allow other people to push you outside them. It might be something as simple as choosing not to give in to your employer's requests for you to work overtime because of how tired it makes you, or choosing not to go to your mother's house if a friend is going to be there who always makes rude comments and makes you feel bad about yourself. Or it might be more serious, such as leaving a relationship that is abusive or requires more of you than you can give. Look at your Loss of Control Action Sheet, see which experiences made you feel a loss of control, and decide where to set your boundaries with those people and experiences.

Suppose you feel the need to set boundaries or end a relationship, but don't feel you have the courage to do so, or feel you need more insight as to what you should do. You can also tap on these issues to help remove blockages that can prevent you from seeing clearly what you should do, or to remove fear so that you can take appropriate action.

Now, let's just recap the procedure.

Suppose you filled out the Loss of Control Action Sheet, and you wrote that one of the events that made you feel a loss of control was when a relationship with a partner ended. You felt lost without them and there was nothing you could do to get them back. You also couldn't get rid of the sad feelings you were experiencing. So you experienced the loss of a significant relationship, and the inability to control your sadness. You probably also felt some hopelessness in this situation. So you can tap on sadness, loss of relationship, hopelessness, and loss of control in general.

First, rate your intensity level. Then go on to do the tapping. If it were me, I'd probably make up some statements like this:

"Even though I am sad about losing Jerry, I still deeply and completely love and accept myself."

"Even though I have not been able to get rid of this sadness, I now choose to feel freer, lighter and happier."

"The sadness is now going away."

"I feel hopeful that my life will be full and happy again."

Now, do the tapping procedure, and then check in on what's going on inside you right now. What would you say your most dominant feeling is at this time? Is it a comfortable or uncomfortable feeling? If it's a feeling you don't want, tap on that.

Rate your intensity level. Is it more or less intense than when you started? Keep going through the process until you feel comfortable with how you are feeling, and the decisions you have made about the boundaries you need to set.

Make a list below of the people or situations that need a boundary, and your decision about what that boundary will be.

Issue	Boundary	When?

_____   _____   _____

_____   _____   _____

_____   _____   _____

_____   _____   _____

_____   _____   _____

_____   _____   _____

What kind of boundaries should I set?

You should always be able to feel that you are in control of your own life and circumstances. Once you start to use ABT to change your thoughts and feelings, you will see that you really **are** the one in control, because if some person or circumstance starts to make you feel stressed, you can help your body to get back into balance, to quickly lower the levels of stress hormones in your blood stream, and quickly change your feelings. You will find that if you use ABT on a daily, consistent basis, it not only helps you recognize situations ahead of time that could cause problems for you, but helps you deal quickly with things that come up so that those things don't fester and start getting your brain chemistry out of balance again.

If you are unsure of what decision to make or what boundary to set, then tap using the phrase, "Even though I am not sure what to do right now, the path I am to take is becoming clearer by the moment." You will be amazed at how this clears away blockages that can keep you from seeing things clearly.

Choose a situation that you know has been uncomfortable for you in the past. What made you uncomfortable in that situation? Did someone say or do something that made you feel threatened? Did you feel that your needs weren't being respected? Did you feel unable to be yourself with that person or situation?

Construct a statement that summarizes what makes you uncomfortable about this person or situation. Then name some boundaries you could set to avoid having these uncomfortable experiences. In my own situation, I might have constructed a statement that said, "When I go to my work each day, I feel sad, trapped and hopeless." The boundaries I might set would be:

I will not do overtime.

Each week I will fill out at least one job application for some other job I would enjoy more.

Each day I will do at least one thing to bring myself closer to self-sufficiency so I don't have to work at this job.

On the weekends I will not spend all my time working around the house or fulfilling other responsibilities, I will spend at least some of the time satisfying my soul with beautiful music, a drive in the country, or something that makes me feel good.

I will give myself something to look forward to, a goal that can be achieved within a relatively short time.

For instance, I always wanted a cobalt-blue Kitchen Aide refrigerator with filtered water and ice in the door. My husband always made fun of the idea. I started saving up for it and within a few months, I had a concrete reminder that I can do anything I want. Anything IS possible!

Now, write down your own boundaries. Even write down the ones that you think of that you're not sure will work. Just write down all ideas that come into your head. You are going to get some intuitive assistance with deciding which ideas will work best in your situation. You will be able to get confirmation that the decisions you are making are right for you.

Getting Confirmation

When trying to make any decision in which there are several alternatives and you don't know which one is right, make a list of the possible decisions. You are going to tap on each one.

Before tapping, rate the intensity of feeling you have about each decision. By that I mean, rate on a scale of 0 to 10, with 10 being the highest, how sure you are that this is the right decision, or how strongly you feel that taking this action is what you should do. Out beside each decision that you have written down, write a number. Just close your eyes and think about that decision, or hold a picture in your mind of yourself doing that thing, and see how strongly you feel about that decision.

In my own case, using the boundaries I listed earlier, the statement "Each day I will do at least one thing to bring myself closer to self-sufficiency so I don't have to work at this job" feels like 6 to me, but "Each week I will fill out at least one job application for some other job I would enjoy more. "

feels like an 8 because it is more concrete, more definable. The others feel like 4's and 5's to me.

Now, you are going to tap on each of these decisions. Start with the karate chop point, and say the whole sentence or group of sentences that describe the decision while continuing to tap on that point. Then give it a prompting phrase like "long visits" or "30 minutes" or whatever fits in your situation.

After you have done one round of tapping, rate your intensity again. Has it gone up or down? Do one more round to see if you can further increase or decrease your intensity. Do this for all the decisions you have written down. At some point, one of the decisions should score higher than all the others. Your body is using all available data to give you guidance about what you should do, such as the level of stress hormones when you think about that decision, how thinking about that decision affects the balance of your energy system, whether or not it moves you closer to a short circuit or not, and other intuitive means of gathering data. Choose the decision with the highest score. Is that a decision you think you can carry out?

If there is one decision that you feel is the right one, but you are unable to get comfortable with the idea of carrying out that decision, tap on your feelings about this. For instance, use the phrase "Even though I like the idea of moving to Colorado, I am afraid to take that big step." You can tap on this several times if you need to, changing the phrase as it feels right to you, until you think you will be able to actually carry it out without undue stress.

As always, take your time with all this. This can take as much or as little time as you need it to. Some people can complete this all in one afternoon, and for some, it will take time. This is no right or wrong amount of time. In general, the changes in your energy system happen pretty quickly when you find the right phrase to tap on.

If there is another person involved in your tapping statements, go talk to them and if you feel comfortable doing it, have them tap along with you while you are repeating your decision. Even if the person doesn't understand why you have made this decision, or doesn't really agree, ask them if they will tap along with you anyway. In my case, if I could get my husband to tap with me on "I will move to Colorado when I am able to find the right employment and pay all my bills," that would be beneficial. Without even knowing it, the person will be balancing their own energy system so that they will feel comfortable doing what you ask.

Even if you don't get the other person to tap, or you don't feel comfortable asking them, you can still do something called **surrogate tapping** in which you tap and say the phrases as if you were the other person. You hold in your mind the idea you want the other person to adopt, and say the phrase as if you were them. Pretend you are your husband and say, "I will not ask my wife to live somewhere that she will be unhappy" or whatever the phrase is. You may not understand why this works, and we could get into a complicated discussion of quantum physics to explain it, but the electrical system of your body interacts constantly with the electrical systems of all the people and things around you.

If you had an electrical field sensor, you could walk up to any electrical appliance in your home, stand in front of it, and the sensor would go off, indicating that it has detected an electrical field. These fields extend out from objects quite a distance, depending on how strong they are. Your body also generates a similar electrical field, it's just more delicate and hard to detect with the same field sensor you would use on an appliance. When a doctor gives you an EEG or EKG test, they are testing the specific electrical field generated by your heart or brain. But your whole body generates an electrical field that interacts at all times with people and objects around you. That's why you can be affected so strongly by people and events around you. So it's not surprising to realize that you yourself can influence the frequency of these fields and the behavior and events that result from them.

What if I need help?

If you are tapping and can't seem to get any results, and you don't have anyone with you that can help give you some perspective, make someone up in your mind. Pretend that you have a friend there with you, or just make up an imaginary person, someone who makes you feel strong and safe. Start talking to the person as if they are there with you. Have a conversation with them in which you discuss what's bothering you. Maybe it's your brother. Say "James, I can't seem to get a handle on this problem. I always feels so sad when I go to work, and I really don't want to be there." Then let James respond in your mind by saying whatever you think he might say back to you. Going through this process of having a conversation with someone who you think is safe and fairly objective can help bring to mind things you might not have considered before.

If you feel you do need a real person to help you with this, we are available to help you over the phone. You can sign up for an online or phone session by calling

The Center for Unhindered Living at 580-483-4767.

Now let's discuss some other positive changes you might consider to help yourself stay healthy and depression-free.

References:

1. Pagel MD, Becker J, Coppel DB. Loss of control, self-blame and depression: an investigation of spouse caregivers of Alzheimer's disease patients. *Journal of Abnormal Psychology* [1985, 94(2):169-82].
2. Seligman, M. *Helplessness*. Freeman: New York, 1992.

CHAPTER NINE

POSITIVE CHANGES TO PREVENT DEPRESSION

The night I began writing this book, I was at the end of my rope. I had just started a business a couple of months earlier, and just after I signed a one year lease on an office space, my husband lost his job. For two months, we had been surviving on the money my new business was bringing in, which wasn't much at first. I had been using the money for only those things we absolutely had to have - food, gasoline and utilities. All our other bills were behind, our cell phones had been turned off because we couldn't pay the bill, Sparkletts had stopped delivering water to our home because I was two months behind in paying them, and we literally didn't know from one day to the next if we were going to have the money to buy groceries.

That night I had gone to the grocery store with $12 in my wallet. It was hard to choose what to buy, knowing we had so many needs. I had to buy light bulbs because we couldn't see to go to the bathroom or walk around the house at night because of no light, so that reduced what I had to spend on food to $10.96. I knew I could buy enough for tomorrow, but that was it. We had been living on Ramen noodles and cereal. I didn't care if it took all the money I had, tonight I was going to buy meat. I put hamburger and chicken nuggets in my cart, and headed for the checkout. As I walked to the front of the store, all I could do was notice what other people had in their carts. I had a bad feeling in the pit of my stomach, and I wanted it to stop. I don't want to feel this way anymore, I thought.

"You have a choice," a voice said.

I looked around. No, it wasn't somebody standing behind me, it was that little voice that often talked to me. You know, that one in your head that you often ignore? I knew what it was trying to say to me, what it always says: that

I have a choice about how to feel. What I think and feel, and how I react, is within my control. It's my choice.

I was irritated with the voice. Standing in the checkout line, I talked back inside my head. "I know it's my choice, and right now I'm choosing to feel lousy because I'm BROKE!"

The voice said, "Well, when you're tired of feeling lousy, you know what to do."

I was even more irritated with voice because it was right. I did know. I was just tired. Tired of going on. I knew things would get better, that we wouldn't always be broke. But what do you do when you are just tired of trying? How do you keep going on?

That's what this book is about. How you can do it, just like I did.
I've always known that I would write a book, maybe more than one. I had started several, but they just never seemed right. Then I started to think about what I could create. It needed to be something that embodied the essence of who I am. It needed to be something unique to me. So I started to think about myself and who I really am, and the first thing that came to me was my unwavering belief that everything will always be all right. That was quite ironic, given my present circumstances. Here I was, feeling at the end of my rope, like I couldn't go on, and still there was something inside me that
wouldn't give up, couldn't give up, never will give up. And so I thought, if there is one gift that I can give the world, it is the knowledge of how to keep going, even when you feel like you can't.

I would encourage you to make one statement a part of your daily ABT tapping routine: "No matter what happens, everything will always turn out all right." Now, you may not believe this, and we could argue all day about whether or not it's even possible, but this is the foundational belief at the core of my being that keeps me from giving up: the belief that at it's most fundamental level, the universe is structured in such a way that things will work out for my greater good, and the greater good of all in the long run.

So whether you believe it or not, tap on that statement every day. It will become ingrained in your being, so that when times are hard, if you've already programmed yourself on a basic energetic level with this idea, you'll always be able to hang on, despite whatever life may throw at you. If you have hope, if you know undoubtedly that there is hope, it can help you stay healthier emotionally.

Tip #1: Believe it will be all right.

Around the time that I was eight years old, I received an important spiritual message. Living in a dysfunctional family, which defined my every waking moment, I was beginning to become self-aware, and recognized that on a fundamental level, I was different. I often didn't understand the things my family said and did. They were often illogical, hurtful, and destructive, without even knowing it. In the midst of this awakening realization that I was to be different, that I didn't want to embrace the kinds of beliefs and behavior I was seeing, I received a message. It was more like a thought, firmly planted in my mind, something that I believed with a firm resolve but had no realistic reason to believe. The message was, "No matter what happens to you, everything will be all right."

As I think about this, years later, I realize that this was NOT a statement that I gradually came to believe or that I always believed on a certain level but gradually came to verbalize. It was a reality that was planted firmly into my consciousness. There was no one in my family that would possibly have planted this idea within me, because my family, my mother in particular, didn't believe this, and I was constantly bombarded with statements about how bad things were and what could happen to me if I didn't watch out. My mother had been traumatized by events in her early life, and as a result, she feared everything. She was always vigilant so she could avoid the bad thing that was coming next. It drained the joy from her life. She was always worried and anxious, and I just didn't see the need to worry that much. Looking back on it now, when I received this message, I experienced it as supernatural. I was a sensitive child, but at the same time, strong. I feel one reason for this was the unwavering nature of the message. I was to believe it unconditionally, and without a doubt. It has become the foundation of my belief system, the essence of who I am. It's why I can keep on going.

You might be thinking, "Yes, but things DON'T always turn out right. Why spend time and energy believing that they will?" Because on a fundamental level, everything that happens, even the negative things, happen for a good reason. Remember when we talked about how the symptoms of depression are really your body trying to protect you from whatever was harming you? Of course, the symptoms are not pleasant, but they have a reason for existing. I realize that whatever you've gone through in your life, the abuse or suffering you've had, is hard to view this way. And if you can't see it that way, I understand. I don't expect anything of you that you can't give. You don't need to try to force yourself to see things this way, but allow for the possibility that someday you can. You might tap on that by saying, "Even though I'm angry about _____ happening to me, I want to see things differently." This allows for the possibility that someday you might change your mind, without forcing you to accept right now what that change will be.

Tip#2: Listen to the voice.

No, this is not the same voice that talks to people who have paranoid delusions. This is just the little inner voice that we all have which nudges us when there is something important we need to know or pay attention to. Pay attention to your gut feelings. These also work on that unseen energetic level, where your body is taking all the biological information it has and is distilling it down into a feeling or intuition that it can make you understand. Your first impressions or gut feelings are most often right, because it's what you feel before you have time to think about it and rationalize as to why what you just thought about couldn't be true. Once your rational mind gets involved, the power of those intuitions or feelings will disappear.

Tip #3: Start Journaling

One of the things that makes us feel like giving up is how disconnected we feel from other people and events in our lives, and even ourselves. A journal helps establish some continuity in your life. It's something you do every day, it's familiar, it becomes like an old friend to you. Even when things are going wrong in your life, your journal is still there. When there's no one to talk to, your journal will listen.

Journaling is more than just writing down what happened to you during the day. It has many positive aspects which can be helpful to you in mental, emotional, and spiritual ways. Journaling is an effective means of stress reduction. By writing about what troubles or frustrates you, this makes it possible for you to release much of those frustrations so you carry less of it with you. Journaling actually helps you to see and understand more clearly what you want and what is important to you. It helps you focus. It also helps you recognize issues to use in your daily tapping sessions.

Routine journaling means making time for you, and this is something people do not do enough of. Setting aside time each day when you give yourself permission to openly examine your thoughts and feelings, and to value what you think and believe, is in and of itself therapeutic. Journaling can enhance intuition and creativity. It awakens your inner voice, helps you learn to trust yourself. It helps you improve your ability to gain insight and sensitivity to things going on both outside and inside yourself. It shifts your perspective so you can understand things differently. It reveals the great potential that is within you, and helps you find more meaning in life.

Journaling can also help you to access the spiritual part of yourself. When you journal, you create a special devotional space, a place that is sacred and holy for you. You can ask your questions, and receive your answers from whatever source you choose: God, angels, the universe, or your inner self. Journaling also helps you begin to see how everything in your life and indeed, in the universe, is connected. You'll begin to notice things that seem to be related, that on the surface appear to be coincidental, but the more you examine them, the more you see that they are most certainly linked. You begin to get a sense that you are part of something bigger than yourself. Now, you just have to discover what that "something" is. Because if there is something out there, something you can be a part of, something that can make your life easier and help you keep going, I know you want to discover what that "something" is.

I also have another book, "The Long and Winding Road" which is a journal with blank pages that contains therapeutic journaling topics for you to write about on a daily basis. You can get the book from Amazon.com or through our website, www.unhinderedliving.com

Tip #4: Create a sacred space

Now give some thought to the sacred space you want to create when you journal. This is your space and your time, what do you want it to be like? It would be perfect if you could find a special place to go when you write in your journal, so you could bless or dedicate that space and make it conducive to productive thinking and feeling. I have a room that I go to, it has two chairs with an end table between them, a small lamp with soft lighting, and a compact disc player for meditative music. The only thing I do in this room is think, meditate, and write, so the room has a special feel to it that no other room has. It's where I ask my questions and find my answers.

Most people aren't going to have a special room they can devote only to journaling, praying, meditating or just thinking, so here are some suggestions for setting aside your own special devotional space:

1. Arrange your bedside table so that it is a backdrop for your special space. You can have a lamp with soft lighting, a small tabletop water fountain, scented candle, and small devotional items that are meaningful to you. Arrange it so that everything on the table is pleasurable to you or meaningful in some way. On my meditative table, I have a green candle (green is the color of growth and healing), a diffuser with essential oils heated by a candle (Frankincense and sandalwood oils are excellent at encouraging a calm, meditative state), a small book of poetry I had once given my mother, who has now passed on (I feel her presence and often ask for her assistance and guidance), a prayer mala made of white jade (for protection), a small statue of a crescent moon overlooking an autumn scene (autumn is my favorite season and this scene

reminds me that to everything there is a season and a purpose), and some beautiful, smooth purple stones. These are the things that are meaningful to me. You can use religious icons, but if you don't want to, simply use a candle and some fresh flowers, or whatever you find pleasing, calming, and peaceful.

2. If your bedside table won't work because you have small children that disturb the objects you place there, or because you don't feel you can be alone and uninterrupted while sitting in your bedroom, the bathroom is an alternative space where you can usually steal a few minutes to be alone. Turn the shower on so the rest of your family will think you are taking a shower and won't disturb you. You can keep a candle in your bathroom cabinet and pull it out whenever you are going to create your sacred space. I turn on the shower, light the candle, turn off the lights, and sit there calmly writing in my journal for fifteen minutes. The sound of the water is also soothing.

3. If the people in your house are noisy or just keep bothering you, take a CD with some peaceful music out to your car, put the music on, and spend fifteen minutes writing in your journal. Let your family members know, when you see mom sitting alone in the car, don't disturb her unless the house is burning down.

4. If you have small children who will sit and listen to a story being read, go to the storytime at your local public library. While your children sit enthralled by the storyteller, you sit with your earphones on, listening to peaceful music and writing in your journal.

5. Find a neighbor who would also like to meditate or journal. Pick a half hour each day when you will each spend fifteen minutes watching the kids play outside so the other can have fifteen minutes to journal (longer if you can swing it).

6. If you are a nursing mom, journal for fifteen minutes each day while your baby is breastfeeding. The prolactin released into your bloodstream while breastfeeding is the

perfect relaxant.

7. If you must commute to your job each day, journal while on the subway, bus or train. You can create your sacred space mentally, anywhere you go. If you have to create your sacred space mentally, sit comfortably, close your eyes, and visualize a beautiful place that makes you feel relaxed, safe, comfortable, and satisfied. Perhaps you visualize sitting on the sand by the ocean, or in a beautiful, luxurious room in a beautiful, soft chair. Perhaps you visualize a place that feels sacred to you. Or, simply draw a circle around yourself in your mind, and state to yourself, "Within this circle, I am safe, loved, blessed, enlightened, and adored." You could visualize sitting in a bright, white bubble, with your angels hovering overhead to protect and comfort you, and make your space a beautiful, loving place. Make it whatever you want it to be.

Tip #5: Choose a personalized aromatherapy oil

Different fragrances have a remarkable ability to uplift and change mood. There is a scientific reason for this, as the different oils have their own energetic frequencies, and the molecules enter the blood stream quickly when inhaled. Japanese companies have found that introducing lemon oil into the air supply of their offices increases productivity and reduces work errors. Studies of lavender oil found that inhaling it increased the speed and accuracy of math computations. If you are not interested in the scientific reasons why essential oils work, there are always the spiritual reasons. In the Bible, fragrant incense was burned in the tabernacle. In many spiritual traditions, incense or fragrant oils are burned as part of a ritual, and these scents help to uplift and empower the individual.

Antidepressant oils: Bergamot, Clary sage, jasmine absolute, lavender, lemon, sweet orange, patchouli, peppermint, rose, rose geranium, rosemary, rosewood, sandalwood, ylang-ylang. Lavender is the preferred favorite in this category.

To help balance mood swings: Bergamot, Grapefruit, Jasmine absolute, juniper, sweet orange, rose, rosewood.

To aid in better sleep: Clary sage, lavender, rose, rose geranium, ylang ylang

To aid with stress and tension: Grapefruit, lavender, rose, rose geranium, rosewood, sandalwood, vanilla, ylang ylang

To reduce anxiety: jasmine absolute, lavender, lemon, sandalwood, ylang ylang

Rejuvenating oils: Lemon, peppermint

Never use these oils on the skin straight without being diluted. Do not ingest the oils unless they are Young Living Therapeutic-grade oils, and only according to package directions.

Suggestions for using the oils:

1. Place a few drops of oils into a bowl of very hot water. Inhale the vapors that rise from the hot water.

2. Use a candle diffuser to heat the oils and scent the room. Fill the top of the candle diffuser with hot water, add 10 drops of oil. You don't have to place this near you, it will diffuse throughout the entire room.

3. Place a few drops of essential oil on a tissue and tuck it inside your blouse or shirt, or in a front pocket.

4. Place a few drops of essential oil in your pillowcase so that you can inhale the scent as you sleep. Lavender is especially relaxing.

5. Place 10-12 drops of oil into a hot bath.

6. Light a candle and put several drops of oil into the hot wax.

7. Add a few drops of oil to your favorite unscented lotion.

8. Get a car diffuser so you can scent your car as well. Or in a pinch, just put a few drops on a cotton ball and hang it from the rear view mirror.

Tip #6: Get your Friends Involved

Having depression can be a very isolating experience, partly because you don't want to be around others, and partly because others don't understand what you are going through. Try to combat this isolation by getting your friends involved. Ask three or four of your closest friends to meet with you. At this meeting, explain to your friends about how depression makes you feel and some things that they could do to help you. Some of those things might be:

1. Ask one of your friends to be available to talk to you on the phone once in a while when you need to let things out. Let your friend know that you do not expect him or her to fix things, just to let you vent your feelings.

2. Ask your friends to email you once a week and just tell you something they like or appreciate about you. Depression hits people harder that have low self-esteem.

3. If you have children, ask your friends to take turns watching your children for just two hours, once a week, so that you can do something you enjoy. It's something to look forward to, and if you have several friends, no one person would have to do it very often.

4. Ask a friend to call you once a week to check on you.

5. Ask a friend to walk, run or workout with you somehow, not only to get you out of the house, but because vigorous exercise causes the body to produce natural endorphins which can help elevate mood. Also, just walking beside a person without talking, the two people fall into the same rhythm and feel a connection with each other that is important. It can help synchronize their minds and moods.

6. Both you and a friend keep a journal. Meet once a week to share excerpts from your journal with each other.

7. Ask a friend to get involved with you in some

volunteer work.

Tip #7: Pet Therapy

According to WebMD, playing with a dog or cat can raise levels of serotonin and dopamine, neurotransmitters that are known to have pleasurable and calming properties. Numerous studies have shown that those who own pets have lower blood pressure, lower levels of stress hormones in the blood, and men that own dogs have shown lower cholesterol levels than those who don't. It can also boost the immune system in numerous ways.

For those with depression, there are many benefits to pet ownership. Pets love unconditionally and don't have the expectations of us that people do. Petting an animal is a pleasurable tactile experience, and the purring of a cat actually has healing qualities. Pets need to be fed, watered and taken for walks or played with, and many people with depression have reported that just knowing their pet needed their care made them get out of bed in the morning. Walking your dog makes you get needed exercise and sunshine. Some depressed people who had contemplated suicide have reported that knowing their pets would probably die if they weren't there to care for them kept them from taking their own lives. Pets give us socialization and keep us from feeling so isolated and alone. They are always there, never complaining but giving back so much genuine affection.

Tip #8 Use Narrative Restructuring

Get a notebook, and make it a priority to design yourself a new life. In this notebook, you are only going to write about your life **as you want it to be.** Write it as if you are creating a fictional story about another character. Write in detail, letting your imagination flow and creating a life that is everything you've ever wished for or imagined. Make it an interesting, creative story. The more you write about it as if it's already a reality, the more it becomes less fiction and more an actual possibility. Live with this story on a daily basis, and then when the opportunity presents itself for you to actually do something that fits in with your story, you'll feel much more comfortable about actually stepping out and doing it, since you've already explored it mentally and emotionally.

Tip #9 Try Ecotherapy

New ecotherapy research from the University of Essex in the UK gives us credible evidence that contact with nature can effect depression. Walks in nature yield better results than anti-depressants. Prisoners with a view of nature are less violent. Mental health of elderly patients improves when a pet or small child comes to visit. Children relax and become cheerful in a school garden. Patients heal faster when a tree is outside their window.

The study by the University of Essex compared the benefits of a 30-minute walk in a country park with a walk in an indoor shopping center. After the country walk, 71% reported decreased levels of depression and said they felt less tense while 90% reported increased self-esteem. This was in contrast to only 45% who experienced a decrease in depression after the shopping center walk, after which 22% said they actually felt more depressed. Some 50% also felt more tense and 44% said their self-esteem had dropped after spending time window shopping.

Combining ecotherapy with ABT can boost the effectiveness of both, in my opinion. Go to a nature spot that you enjoy. Sit next to the babbling brook or where you can watch the animals. Watch a beautiful sunset. After you have chosen a spot that feels comfortable and relaxing to you, do some deep breathing exercises. With each exhale, let go of any stress you might be feeling. Pay attention to how being in nature makes you feel, how integrated you feel with the rest of your surroundings. Especially notice how in this environment, there are no expectations of you, there are no pressures, and everything seems right. Start doing your tapping to get rid of some negative issues and replace them with positive feelings.

"Even though I feel my job is too stressful and my family doesn't understand me, out here I feel comfortable and free."

"Even though my _____ issues make me feel uncomfortable, sad and angry, I can let go of those feelings here." (Even if you don't think you can, go ahead and say it.)

"Even though I'm afraid of _____ , when I am in this place, anything seems possible."

"When I am in this place, I can receive energy and strength to go on."

"When I am in this place, I finally feel that I belong somewhere."

You might take your journal with you, and write down all the phrases that come to you which embody how you feel. Of course, if you would like to move to the country and are able to, that would be great. But if you can't, take some of this energy and strength back with you to your regular life. Get a container: a pretty basket, or wooden box, a pretty glass jar, whatever appeals to you. Take a walk in your countryside and place some items in your container that will remind you of your visit: a river rock, a shell, some acorns, a pine cone, some leaves from a tree, whatever you find in that environment. Take your container full of items back with you and place them in your home so that when you feel stressed or upset, you can see, touch, smell and handle those things which will remind you of the calm peacefulness you experienced in nature.

Tip #10 Try Art Therapy

Pick a medium and start expressing yourself. You don't have to be good at it, just going through the process is the most important thing. Using art to express yourself often results in increased feelings of self-awareness and awareness of others, helps you cope with the effects of stress and traumatic experiences, and gives you a voice when you feel you have none. It can be very helpful and extremely satisfying. The list of mediums is endless: painting, sculpting, woodworking, steel artwork, drawing and sketching, ceramics, pottery, photography, digital media, collage, chalk/pastels, weaving, dancing, singing, making clothing, glass art, jewelry making, and much more. Perhaps you will come up with your own innovative medium. If nothing else, get a box of crayons, and get started!

Tip #11 What if the issue behind your depression is an illness you feel powerless to change?

If that's the case, you really need ABT more than ever, because it has been shown to be helpful in dealing with the physical symptoms of disease as well as emotional issues. Physical pain responds well to electrical stimulation, and some people even have complete elimination of whatever their physical problem is after they deal with the emotional issues associated with it.
Yes, we've had people with all the following diseases report significant improvement in their condition after using ABT:

Addictions
Allergies
Asthma
Headaches
Vision Problems
Blood Pressure
Diabetes
Carpel Tunnel

Eating disorders
Multiple Sclerosis
Parkinson's
Fibromyalgia
Baby's colic
Indigestion
Back pain
Sleep Disorders
Low blood platelets
Bedwetting
Skin disorders
Yeast symptoms
ADD/ADHD
Arthritis
Vertigo
Tinnitus
Epileptic seizures
Cancer
Lupus
Miscellaneous Infections
Conjunctivitis
Leukemia
The common cold

Tip #12 Check Your Diet

Many people with depression find that one of three things affects their depression significantly:

1. Low blood sugar
2. Pesticides on foods
3. A specific food allergy

If you are using ABT and are finding that it helps you in the short term, but the depression seems to come back again, continue to use the ABT to get rid of your daily symptoms, but try to eliminate the root cause. Keep a journal of the times when the depression comes back. Write down anything that you were exposed to right before you experienced the recurrence. What did you eat? What did you drink? Did you brush your teeth or use specific personal care products? Where you exposed to any cleaning products? Often people will find that they ate a specific food right before the depression began. If you ate an apple right before you got depressed, stop eating apples for 24 hours. Then eat another one and see if that is the culprit. If it happens again, eliminate apples again for another 24 hours, then eat an ORGANIC apple that contains no pesticides. Then you will find out if it's the apple, or what's been sprayed on the apple. Try eating small meals every couple of hours. If it's hypoglycemia, or low blood sugar, this should help. Some people find that when their blood sugar drops extremely low, their depression returns. You could get a blood sugar monitoring device and actually test your blood sugar if you wanted to so you could get an idea which foods help stabilize your blood sugar most effectively. A normal blood sugar two hours after a meal ought to be somewhere around 100 or so.

ABT Tapping Phrases that Work

"Even though I am not happy in my work, I thoroughly and completely love, accept and forgive myself."

"Even though insensitive people get me down, I thoroughly and completely love myself unconditionally."

"Even though there are dark clouds hanging over me, I choose to believe the sun will shine through those dark clouds."

"Despite the fact that my mother treats me disrespectfully, I am still a great person."

"Even though the people at my church treat me as a sinner, I know God accepts me."

"Although some things at my job are causing me stress, I am able to perform my job with joy."

"Even though people disagree with me, I can let it go."

"Even though I have this headache pain, I accept myself as a loving, decent person."

"Despite the fact that I sometimes get angry at my husband, I feel calm and in control."

"Even though I don't have enough money for next month's rent, at the present moment I am safe and sound, and am at peace.

"Even though my blood pressure is too high, I feel calm and restful."

"Even though my blood sugar has been too high in the past, my body is now processing the sugar appropriately."

"I feel peaceful and calm no matter how my child behaves."

"Even though I hate the man who abused me, I thoroughly and completely love, accept and forgive myself."

"Even though I have this major depression, I thoroughly and completely love, accept and forgive myself."

"Despite the fact that I don't believe there is any treatment that can help me, I am feeling better about my condition."

Is there anything else we can help you with?

We have many, varied methods to help you with your life issues. The Accu-Balancing Technique can be combined with other life-changing self-help techniques to design a program that addresses your individual, personal needs. Other services we offer, both in person, by phone and through internet conference room are:

ABT FOR PETS
AWARE PARENTING
THE SEDONA METHOD
PERSONAL COACHING
STRESS MANAGEMENT
ANGER MANAGEMENT
MEDITATION TRAINING
SPIRITUAL DEVELOPMENT
NUTRITION CONSULTATION
ABT FOR PAIN IN CHILDBIRTH
FAMILY EFFECTIVENESS TRAINING
COMPLETE CHILDBIRTH EDUCATION
HOW TO ATTAIN FINANCIAL FREEDOM
REIKI TREATMENTS AND ATTUNEMENT
FENG SHUI WORKSHOPS AND CONSULTATIONS

Call us today if we can help with any other life issues.

CHAPTER TEN

APPENDIX

Contact Information for
The Center for Unhindered Living

580-483-4767
unhinderedliving@gmail.com

Personal Bill of Rights

Every man, woman, and child has the following rights by virtue of the fact that they exist. These are reasonable and ordinary expectations, which create appropriate boundaries.

I have the right to make my own choices.

I have the right to follow my own values and standards, as long as I am not abusive towards others.

I have a right to dignity and respect.

I have a right to all of my feelings.

I have a right to express myself as long as I am not abusive toward others.

I have a right to determine and honor my own priorities.

I have a right to recognize and accept my own value system as appropriate.

I have a right to have my needs and wants respected by others.

I have the right to say no when I feel I am not ready, unsafe, or that it violates my values (this goes for kids too...they have the right to say "no" to their parents)

I have the right to make mistakes and not have to be perfect.

I have the right not to be responsible for others behavior, actions, feelings or problems.

I have a right to be uniquely me, without feeling I'm not good enough.

I have the right to make decisions based on my feelings and judgment for any reason.

I have the right to change my mind at any time.

I have the right to my personal space and time needs.

I have the right to be flexible and be comfortable with doing so.

I have the right to be in a safe, non-abusive environment.

I have the right to forgive others and forgive myself.

I have the right to give and receive unconditional love.

I have the right to enjoy being sexual and celebrate my sexuality.

I have the right to my own spiritual beliefs and to celebrate them.

I have the right to grieve when I don't get what I need.

I have the right to grieve when I get something I didn't need or want.

I have the right to joyfully receive without feeling guilty.

I have a right to healthy relationships of my choice.

I have the right to be angry with someone I love.

I can take care of myself, no matter what.

I have the right to be, and can be, healthier than those around me.

I have the right to trust others who earn my trust.

I have the right to terminate conversations for any reason.

It is OK to be relaxed, playful and frivolous.

I have a right to expect honesty from others.

I have the right to change and grow.

I have the right to follow my own path.

I have the right to be happy.

The Devastating Role of Religion in Mental Health

Throughout my life as a Christian and as a mental health professional, the devastating role that religion plays in the development of unhealthy thoughts and beliefs has become evident. My efforts to help people overcome their unhealthy mental and emotional habits are often hampered by the person's religious convictions. Not only can people not heal from emotional stress and trauma when embracing religious ideas that keep them in bondage, but these religious ideas themselves are often the cause of the stress and trauma.

I am not trying to say that no one should embrace a religious faith. That is for each person to decide. But you can choose to embrace a faith that is not toxic and does not lead you to accept an unhealthy, emotionally debilitating state as normal. Here are some of the "ideas" which have no basis in fact but that are taught to people as "truth" and which hold people in bondage:

Humans are born with a sinful nature. We are basically evil and need to be saved – There is no scientific basis for this claim. A person is not born good or bad. A person learns how to behave through observations of how others behave, and by adapting his responses to try and avoid unpleasant stimuli. There is nothing inherently evil in the individual.

We are not acceptable the way we are – this is the most devastating belief system to buy into, and is the basis of most mental and emotional problems. Because we exist, we have value. Our value is not based upon our behavior or beliefs. Each and every person has equal merit and an equal right to happiness.

People will only do what is right if there is a threat of punishment for doing wrong – First of all, what is "right" is a matter of opinion so it is ludicrous for one person to hold another person to their own standard. Even if you belong to a religious group, what is considered right or wrong depends upon the values of the group and does vary from group to group. Not all churches or religions believe the same thing, hence you cannot trust the group to tell you what is right. It must come from within you. Secondly, all punishment does is destroy the one being punished, it does not improve or build up. It does not make a person more emotionally healthy to endure punishment. On the contrary, it causes a decline in all observable measures of mental health.

I am not capable of doing good. Only God can help me "be good." - This takes the responsibility for changing your life out of your hands and puts it into God's, which is a mistake. You and only you can change your life. All the tools you need to do this are available to you. Perhaps you don't understand how to use them yet, but they are available. Don't give your power and responsibility over to someone else. I know you may be in a hard place right now and you think you have tried everything you know, and you want to turn to someone else who can make all your problems go away, but that is not reality. I don't want you to give up – there are tools out there to help you – but I also don't want you to put your faith in something that does not exist in order to solve your problems. You ARE capable of being and doing good. You CAN get better using the tools that are available.

No one is good, only God – well, how do you define "good"? In reference to God, most people say that he is perfect, sinless and doesn't make mistakes. Well, that doesn't hold water. Throughout the Bible God lied, instructed others to lie, and performed many deceptions. I wouldn't call that good or perfect. For instance, Exodus 5:1 says that God told Moses to speak to Pharaoh and tell him that the Israelites wanted to be allowed to go into the wilderness to celebrate a festival to the Lord. In reality, they were to escape from Egypt and run away. God instructed them to lie. This sort of thing occurs over and over in the Bible. So don't make God's behavior in the Bible our standard for what is right.

If things don't turn out right in my life, there is something wrong with me, not something wrong with God – we are human, we make mistakes, but that does not mean there is something wrong with us. Mistakes are an important part of the learning process and should not be discouraged. Making a mistake is nothing you need to apologize for and doesn't make you unacceptable. People need to consider that maybe their belief system about God is wrong. But we always want to blame ourselves. There is no need for blame of oneself or anyone else. Blame, guilt and shame are not healthy.

It's ok to doubt. In John 20, Thomas told Jesus he would not believe without proof, and Jesus gave him proof that satisfied him. There is nothing wrong with expecting that the things you believe be provable and have evidence to back them up. If you are to believe Jesus, proof is important. Don't accept something you are asked to believe without proof of its veracity. If God says he will give you assistance in time of trouble, and you have prayed and pleaded and no help came, that is proof. Proof that not everything you have been told about God is true. It is reasonable to expect that everything in the Bible, if it is true, WORKS in everyday life. If you have done what the Bible says and it did not work in everyday life, then it is false. You don't have to believe it.

Studies have shown that clergy, and not trained psychological counselors, are most often consulted when a person has an emotional or mental illness. And yet, studies also show that in 32% of cases where a pastoral counselor was consulted, the person asking for help was told they did not really have a mental illness, and were told that the problem was just spiritual in nature. The study also found that women were more likely than men to have their mental health claims dismissed, and that this happened more frequently in fundamentalist churches than more liberal ones. All the participants in this study had already been previously evaluated by a licensed mental health professional and given diagnoses such as bipolar disorder or schizophrenia before approaching the church for assistance. This study was done at Baylor University and was published in the journal *Mental Health, Religion and Culture* (1).

The problem is not just the way the mentally ill are treated but the way religious beliefs interfere with normal cognitive processes. In 1980, Albert Ellis, the founder of rational emotive therapy, wrote in the *Journal of Consulting and Clinical Psychology* that there was an irrefutable causal relationship between religion and emotional and mental illness. According to Canadian psychiatrist Wendall Watters, "Christian doctrine and liturgy have been shown to discourage the development of adult coping behaviors and the human to human relationship skills that enable people to cope in an adaptive way with the anxiety caused by stress" (2).

In 2008 Marcia Webb et al. From Seattle Pacific University conducted a study entitled "Representation of Mental Illness in Christian Self-Help Bestsellers." The study looked at the themes provided in Christian self-help books and how they characterize those with mental illness. The team found that most of these themes focused on depression. "Demonic possession was the most frequently cited reason for depression. Other reasons included negative cognitions, failure as a Christian, and negative emotions. Christian responses to depression were trusting God, religious activity, and individual willpower" (3). An online study of both Protestants and Catholics by Baylor University in 2007 showed that approximately one third of the participants reported that their churches believed their mental illness to be the result of personal sin and another one third had been told that they did not actually have a mental illness even though a mental health professional had diagnosed them (4). Kay Redfield Jamison's 1995 book "An Unquiet Mind" chronicled her struggle with bipolar disorder and how her church treated her. She states that after her book came out

I received thousands of letters from people…many were exceedingly

hostile. A striking number said that I deserved my illness because

I was insufficiently Christian and that the Devil had gotten hold of me.

More prayer, not medication, was the only answer" (5).

In many of the self-help books, Jesus is portrayed as "the Savior who frees people from bondage." If this is the case, why has he turned his back on so many of his people who have repeatedly prayed and trusted him to free them?

If you remember our previous discussion of the factors that lead to depression, you will remember that loss of control and learned helplessness coupled with blame and guilt often invoke depression. What greater guilt could be placed upon someone than to tell them that their personal sin is what is causing their depression, or that their failure to be "Christian enough" is the cause? If their personal sin is the cause, and Jesus took their sin away, it stands to reason that they would no longer be plagued by anything caused by that sin. Yet many devout Christians who have devoted their lives to Christ continue to experience depression. It is a huge injustice for those people to be made to believe that the depression is their fault.

I want those of you who may have experienced this treatment to know that I understand that you have probably tried everything you can think of to get rid of your depression and you have gotten no results or only temporary results. I do not blame you for this. You have done the best you could. Please don't embrace the blame and guilt that others try to place upon you. Earlier in the book we talked about boundaries. I urge you to create a boundary for your own mental sanity that will not allow those who believe such things to be around you. You need to surround yourself with positive messages, not messages of blame, guilt and sin. You now have a tool that can help you that does not rely on the supernatural. If there is a God that exists, then he created the electrical system in your body. The physical laws of science operate within that system. There is a logical explanation for what has happened to you and it can be fixed. Don't allow others to blame you for that. If you were in the same room with someone that had a cold and you caught a cold too, would you blame yourself? No....it's a virus that has invaded your body. It's not sin! In the same way, you have a disruption in your body's energy system. Also not sin! It was at one time believed that epileptics were demon possessed because they writhed about and foamed at the mouth. We now know that epilepsy is a medical condition and is treatable. We don't have to believe in superstitions. Your depression does not have a spiritual cause.

White et al. (1995) found that those who scored higher on a test intended to measure positive feelings about Christianity also scored high in schizotypal personality traits. One of those traits is "magical thinking" that influences behavior, and another is unusual perceptual experiences, bodily illusions, and auditory or visual hallucinations. I'm not saying everyone in your church has schizotypal personality traits, but certainly the leaders who perpetuate the doctrines of the church and stand before you claiming supernatural power are candidates for this diagnosis, and they are the ones propagating the idea that all you have to do is pray enough or in the right way and you will be magically healed of your depression.

According to Dr. M.D. Magee in "The Social Psychology of Christianity",

> In human history, schizotypals are metamagical thinkers, the shamans, the medicine men, the witch doctors, whom anthropologist, Paul Radin described as "half mad", and "healed madmen". Shamans tend to be solitary, talk with the dead, speak in tongues, ride on the moon, and turn into a hyena by night...schizotypal shamanism is, a milder, more controlled version of schizophrenia. Shamans are honoured, if feared members of society, that society wants, and will tolerate the occasional schizophrenic to have. Schizotypalism is at the heart of religion. Who hears a voice in a burning bush? Who sees visions of dead men, and hears them addressing them? Who thinks they speak for God?(6)

I'm not saying every religious person is schizotypal. Not everyone in churches claims to be able to speak in tongues, see visions, hear God's voice, or do miracles (although many churches claim you should be able to). But at some point in time, some schizotypal person with magical thinking claimed to have a message from God, and convinced others he had. And the rest of humanity followed him like he was a pied piper because we all want to believe in something. Something that gives us power, strength, and help. If you have believed in this in the past, I'm not blaming you, because half the world has followed the same path, all I am saying now is WAKE UP!

Perhaps this is something you should tap on. "Even though my belief and devotion to God should have healed my depression, and it hasn't, I thoroughly and completely love, accept and forgive myself." See how good it feels to say this. There is nothing wrong with you as a person because you have this illness. You are worthy. You are good. You have unrecognized power within you. You are a compassionate and loving person. You want to do what is right. You don't deserve to be put down. You are enough.

References:

1. Ellis A. Psychotherapy and atheistic values: a response to A. E. Bergin's "Psychotherapy and religious values." *J Consult Clin Psychol.* 1980;48:635-639.

2. Watters WW. *Deadly Doctrine: Health, Illness and Christian God-Talk.* Buffalo: Prometheus Books; 1992.

3. Webb M., Stetz K., and Hedden K. (2008). Representation of mental illness in Christian self-help bestsellers. *Journal of Mental Health, Religion and Culture.* Vol. 11 no. 7, 697-717.

4. Stanford, M. (2007). Demon or disorder: A survey of attitudes toward mental illness in the Christian Church. *Mental Health, Religion and Culture.* 10(5): 445-449.

5. Jamison, K.R. (2006). The many stigmas of mental illness. *The Lancet,* 367, 533-34.

6. Magee, M.D. (2008). *The Social Psychology of Christianity.* Oct. 25, 2006. Available online: http://www.askwhy.co.uk/truth/324Psychology.php

Mindfulness as a Coping Technique

Mindfulness is a state of being wherein one is aware of all one's thoughts, feelings and sensory experiences in the present moment, without judgment. Mindfulness can easily be combined with the ABT technique, but is beneficial in and of itself alone. . Teasdale, Segal, and Williams (1995) proposed that the skills of attentional control taught in mindfulness meditation could be helpful in preventing relapse of major depressive episodes. Their information-processing theory of depressive relapse suggests that individuals who have experienced major depressive episodes are vulnerable to recurrences whenever mild dysphoric states are encountered because these states may reactivate the depressive thinking patterns present during the previous episode, or episodes, thus precipitating a new episode.

How can mindfulness be helpful? Mindfulness skills will help you focus on one thing at a time in the present moment. By doing this, you can better control and soothe your overwhelming emotions. Mindfulness will also help you learn to identify and separate judgmental thoughts from your experiences. These judgmental thoughts often fuel your overwhelming emotions. Mindfulness can also help you develop something called wise mind – the ability to make healthy decisions about your life based on your rational thoughts and emotions (1).

It's best to start practicing mindfulness when you are calm and the stakes are low. The time to learn to use a new skill is NOT when you are upset about something. Learning to use mindfulness now, when you are calm, will make it easier to remember how to use the skills when you are in the middle of emotional turmoil. Also, the inherent peacefulness of the mindful state is very attractive. Once you have experienced it, you will want to return to that state over and over, and it becomes a haven or sanctuary for you when you feel stressed or are thinking disturbed thoughts.

Let's talk about some exercises that can help introduce you to mindfulness skills.

Attention To a Thing

Choose an object that is in the room with you. Sit comfortably in a chair and have a pad of paper and a pen or pencil handy. If you have a timer or stopwatch, set if for five minutes. During this five minutes, I want you to give your complete attention to this object. What color is it? How does the surface feel? Is it cold? Rough? Soft? Smooth? How many surfaces does it have? Is it heavy or light? Are there any imperfections in the surface? For five minutes, pay attention only to the object and write down everything about it that you can observe. During this time, your mind may wander. Other thoughts may come into your head that have nothing to do with the object, stray thoughts like "What am I going to fix for dinner?" or "Why did my spouse speak to me angrily this morning?" If you have stray thoughts, it's perfectly acceptable. That's what the mind does. As these thoughts enter your mind, acknowledge them and let them go, bringing your focus back to the object you are examining. Acknowledge these thoughts without judgment. The purpose of the exercise is to keep your mind on the object in front of you, but don't berate yourself if you have stray thoughts. They are going to come. Just let the thought go and go back to examining the object. When you have completed this five minute exercise, come back to this book and continue reading.

Attention to Your Thoughts

Now get a clean sheet of paper and try to record all the stray thoughts that came into your mind while you were examining the object. Can you remember them all? There were probably quite a few, and if you don't remember them all, that's Ok. Just write down as many as you can think of. Are there some thoughts you had that you can't remember? That would be normal. Of the ones you do remember, how many of them were really important issues and how many were just stray thoughts that weren't very important? Why do you think your mind was bringing up unimportant stray thoughts in addition to the really important ones? And why was it doing this while you were trying to concentrate on the object? One very simple reason: That's what the mind does. Have you ever experienced a thought popping into your head unbidden which is totally unrelated to what you were thinking about? It happens all the time. So if you can't focus on the object without the stray thoughts, that is ok. It's normal for our minds to flit from one thing to the next. Nobody is mindful without practicing and learning to be mindful.

Mindfulness doesn't mean closing out all thoughts unrelated to the focus of your attention, because that is impossible. There is no need to berate yourself for something that is a normal and natural mental process. What you can do is learn to release the thoughts non-judgmentally.

<u>Using an Anchor</u>

When you are practicing mindfulness, it is helpful to choose an anchor to return to when your mind wanders. Your anchor can be anything. There are three types of learning styles: visual, auditory and kinesthetic. If you are a visual learner, you may be more comfortable with holding a picture of an object in your mind, or actually stare at the object. If you are an auditory learner, you might prefer a chant or mantra, the sound of a metronome clicking, the sound of a watch ticking, or the sound of your breathing. If you are a kinesthetic learner, you might prefer the feeling of the breath going in and out of your lungs, or the feeling of rocking in a rocking chair. Choose whatever is comfortable for you. Get comfortable in your chair or on the floor. Close our eyes. Hold in your mind the thing you have chosen as your anchor. When your mind wanders, simply bring your attention back to the anchor, without judgment about how well or how badly you are doing the process. There's actually no way to do it badly. In mindfulness we don't make moral judgments. Something is either skillful or unskillful. We don't use the terms "good" and "bad."

Set your timer for fifteen minutes. Simply hold the anchor in your mind, or continue to chant, or focus on your breathing, for fifteen minutes. As the stray thoughts come up, gently release them and go back to focusing on the anchor. See how good it feels to know that you are doing it skillfully. See how good it feels to be able to gently let go of those thoughts. Even if the same thought returns over and over, that's all right. It's more important to know how to release it than it is to keep the thought from happening. It's more important to be ok with whatever comes up instead of struggling to make something happen. Just release, and go on. Release, and go on. Start now.

Why is Mindfulness Important?

Most of us spend very little time in the present moment. We spend time worrying about what will happen in the future, or rehashing things that happened to us in the past. We do not know what the future will bring, and we cannot change the past, so living in them is futile. Let's say you are worried you won't be able to pay your rent next month, and you are berating yourself because you spent too much money last month when you should have saved it. Suppose a friend asks you to come over and do something fun but you can't because you are too worried about what might happen in the future to enjoy it. This is causing you stress. One of the symptoms of depression is not getting enjoyment out of things you used to enjoy. In this particular situation, this lack of enjoyment is being caused by you focusing on the past and future. But think about this present moment. In this moment, everything is OK. In the present moment, you have a roof over your head and you are not really in distress. There is nothing negative or dangerous happening to you right now. That is being created by you in your mind. In the present moment, it doesn't exist. If you are mindful of the present moment, you can enjoy whatever is available for your enjoyment now, because the past and future don't exist. This releases stress.

Now, I'm not suggesting that you should ignore the fact that you don't have rent money, you can come up with some strategies for tackling that later. For right now, to make you feel better and to ward off depression, allow yourself to be mindful of how wonderful the present moment is and give yourself permission to enjoy it. When those thoughts of doom come, gently release them. Don't make yourself feel bad for having them. They are a normal part of being human. Just choose an anchor, and come back to focusing on the anchor. Perhaps focus on something you really enjoy, like sitting by the ocean and listening to the waves, or listening to a beautiful piece of music. If you feel guilty for enjoying the music, acknowledge that and gently bring your focus back to the piece of music. If you feel sad, acknowledge that and gently bring your focus back to the music. We would all like to go through our lives without feeling negative emotions, but that's not reality. It's more important to be able to come back to the anchor after you've felt them.

References:

1. McKay, M., Wood, J.C., and Brantley, J. The *Dialectical Behavior Therapy Skills Workbook*. New Harbinger: Oakland, California, 2007.

Letting Go of Attachments

One of the things that can cause problems in our lives is our expectations. Our daily lives have a rhythm and a flow which we should pay attention to. Let's say you are learning to play the piano. You are involved in intense practice every day. Three days a week, you have a great practice. You hit everything right on the money and feel great about the music you produced and about the technical aspects of your performance. Two days a week you might have a practice that is good, but not spectacular. The other two days of the week might be very mediocre and you were not pleased with your progress at all. You might have had things happening in your life that posed an inner struggle for you and caused your performance to be off. It is virtually impossible to live on the mountaintop every day. Accept this. Your life has an ebb and flow and you are not going to feel good every moment. Realize it is not permanent and that things will change. This is a good place to insert some tapping with the phrases:

"Despite the fact that I am not happy with how I have performed today, I accept my performance as a natural and normal part of the rhythm of my life."

"Even though I didn't do well on my test today, I accept the fact that my mistakes will ultimately contribute to an increase in my knowledge."

"No matter how hard it is for me to see how things will work out, I accept the fact that everything is all right in this present moment.

"Even though work was hard today, I realize that smoother times are coming."

"Despite the fact that my mother doesn't understand me, I am still ok."

And here's a great one....

"Even though I am not attached to any outcome, I am free to enjoy and create the life I really want."

Attachments usually get in the way of us getting what we really want because they involve fear, rigidity and other emotional states that push our goals further away, out of our reach. If we are attached to a particular outcome, we might close ourselves off from getting what we really want in some way other than what we had envisioned. For example, if what you really want is to feel happy, and you think that the only way to do this is to never feel sad, you might push your goal of being happy away by not realizing that acknowledging and accepting all of your feelings, even the sad ones, are the pathway to releasing them so you CAN feel happy. Being unwilling to feel and truly own your sadness, keeps you sad. Being willing to feel and truly own your sadness means you accept it and don't try to flee from it. Recognize that sadness is a normal part of life, is temporary, and does not in any way imply that you are weak. It's a normal part of the path.

Think about being happy. Why is it that you think you can't be happy? Usually people say, "Because my life is not the way I want it be." Then you are attached to the outcome. How about saying, "I can be happy no matter what is going on in my life, because my happiness does not depend on things going right." But how do you do that? I realize you can't see a way to believe that you can be happy even though things aren't going like you want. That's when you need to tap....

"Even though I have not yet reached my goals, I am still happy in the present moment." Tap on this every, single day. Find something within yourself that you can accept just the way it is. Maybe you don't' like your hair, your weight, your job, your car, your partner, or lack thereof. What CAN you like? "I like the fact that I do not give up." Or "I like the fact that I allow myself to grieve." Or "I like the fact that I can appreciate my cat." Or "I like the fact that I am a loving human being." Or "I like the fact that I can make good coffee." Find something to appreciate every hour of the day if you have to. Make a list and keep it with you, maybe making it part of your journaling every day.

Mindfulness Cards

Earlier we talked about having an anchor to which you bring your attention back during mindfulness Anything you can use to help you remember to take a few minutes out of your day to be mindful will be helpful. I once read about a busy doctor who wanted a way to remind himself to stop and be mindful for a few minutes throughout the day. He was constantly looking at his watch to make sure he was still on schedule throughout the day, so he got some of those small sticky dots and placed a little green dot on the face of his watch. Then when he looked at his watch, he would remember to be mindful. He would close his eyes, take a slow, deep breath, and relax his shoulders. That's it. Then he would open his eyes and go about his day. After doing this for a while, he realized that he needed to do this more often. So he also put a green dot on every clock in every room of his office, because if he wasn't looking at his watch he was also looking at other clocks. He eventually put the green dot on every doorknob in his office. So before he opened the door to go into each examining room, he'd stop for a few seconds of mindfulness. He found this very helpful in helping him alleviate the stress of the day.

I have developed a tool to help myself be mindful and reduce stress, and thought I would share it with you. They are called Mindfulness Cards. Each card has a word on one side, and the words describe different attributes of mindfulness. I keep the cards in my purse, and everywhere I go during the day, I stop and pull one out. For example, if I have had a stressful day at work, I walk to my car to go home, close and lock the car door, maybe even turn on the air conditioning so it can start cooling off. Then I pull out the deck of cards. I shuffle the cards and randomly select one without looking. The card I pull out says "Perfect Peace." Ah, just what I needed to hear. Just what I want. I will either hold the card between my palms, or set the card up on the dashboard, or someplace else that it is visible. For me, I prefer to hold it between my palms. I then close my eyes, take some deep breaths, relax my body, and use the thought of perfect peace as my anchor. When my mind flits away, back to the cares of the day, I simply acknowledge those thoughts and return to the feeling of perfect peace. I sit there, enjoying the feeling of perfect peace, as long as I want and then open my eyes and drive home.

But what if I had gotten a different card, say "Appreciation." It might be difficult to imagine appreciating the tough circumstances I just left behind at work, but that's not what I'm asking you to do. I'm just asking you to experience appreciation. It doesn't **have** to be appreciation for what happened at work, it can just be a feeling of appreciation for anything in your life, or just the feeling of appreciation itself. Imagine sitting there experiencing the glow you get when you are appreciating something. It still brings inner peace.

Now, I have also been known to get the deck of cards, go through them and grab the Perfect Peace card out of the middle of the deck and use that if it's what I think I need. You can certainly do that. I also find, however, that the unexpected nature of the card I pick when I am doing it randomly is almost like a revelation. It challenges me to experience the spaciousness, depth, or acceptance that is available if I just look beneath the surface.

Some have asked me, "Why do you need a card, why not just think about perfect peace?" That's a good point, and if you want to do this, you can. I find the card simply helps reinforce my focus. Of course the card has no power itself, but my mind gives it the weight of the anchor. Try it, you'll see.

In the pages that follow I have printed the cards for you so that you can cut them out. I would suggest gluing each one to a 3 x 5 index card so they will be sturdier. If you really like the cards, a nice deck is available from our Unhindered Living website. I have also given you a couple of blanks so you can write in a word or two of your own if there is some particular word that is helpful to you.

Spaciousness

Attunement

Grace

Recognition

Flow

Resting

Depth

Warmth

Infinite

Unrestrained

Revealed

Continuous

Ardent

Connection

Transform

Yes

Completion

Observe

Surrender

Appreciation

Acceptance

Perfect Peace

Awaken

Boundless

Grounded

Safe

Enough

Shift

Join

Skillful

Perception

Content

Wonder

Satisfying

Recommended Reading List

Siegel, Ronald D. *The Mindfulness Solution: Everyday Practices for Everyday Problems.* Guilford Press, 2010.

Kabat-Zinn, Jon. *Guided Mindfulness Meditation Series 1.* (CD Set) Sounds True, 2005.

Jamison, Kay. *An Unquiet Mind: A Memoir of Moods and Madness.* New York: Vintage, 1997.

Brach, Tara. *Radical Self-Acceptance.* (CD set) Sounds True, 2005.

Hastings, Sean and Rosenberg, Paul. *God Wants You Dead.* Vera Verba, 2007.

Kabat-Zinn, Jon. *The Mindful Way through Depression.* Guilford Press, 2007.

McMath, Judie. *The Long and Winding Road.* Amazon, 2012.

Craig, Gary. *The EFT Manual.* Energy Psychology Press, 2011.

McKay, Matthew, Wood, Jeffrey and Brantley, Jeffrey. *Dialectrical Behavior Therapy Skills Workbook.* New Harbinger Publications, 2007.

ABOUT THE AUTHOR

Judie C. McMath has a Bachelor's Degree in Psychology and a Minor in Music as well as a Bachelor's Degree in Holistic Nutrition. She also has a Master's Degree in Behavioral Science. She is a certified ABT Practitioner, Behavioral Health Rehabilitation Specialist, Feng Shui Consultant, Reiki Master and Ordained Minister. She is married to Eldon McMath and is the former Unschooling mother of two grown boys, Joshua and Ethan.

www.ingramcontent.com/pod-product-compliance
Lightning Source LLC
Chambersburg PA
CBHW070549290526
45790CB00002B/611

* 9 7 8 1 5 0 7 8 8 4 3 2 4 *